Bernard Moses

The Establishment of Municipal Government in San Francisco

Bernard Moses

The Establishment of Municipal Government in San Francisco

ISBN/EAN: 9783744662581

Printed in Europe, USA, Canada, Australia, Japan

Cover: Foto ©Suzi / pixelio.de

More available books at **www.hansebooks.com**

The Establishment of Municipal Government

IN

SAN FRANCISCO

JOHNS HOPKINS UNIVERSITY STUDIES

IN

HISTORICAL AND POLITICAL SCIENCE

HERBERT B. ADAMS, Editor

History is past Politics and Politics present History — *Freeman*

SEVENTH SERIES

II-III

The Establishment of Municipal Government

IN

SAN FRANCISCO

BY BERNARD MOSES, Ph. D.

Professor of History and Politics in the University of California

---

BALTIMORE

PUBLICATION AGENCY OF THE JOHNS HOPKINS UNIVERSITY

February and March, 1889

JOHN MURPHY & CO., PRINTERS,
BALTIMORE.

THE ESTABLISHMENT

OF

MUNICIPAL GOVERNMENT IN SAN FRANCISCO.

The events associated with the establishment of a municipal government in San Francisco extend over three quarters of a century, from the foundation of the Spanish pueblo, in 1776, to the adoption of the city charter passed by the first legislature of the State of California, in 1851. Within this time it is possible to observe three somewhat clearly defined periods. The first is the period of Spanish settlement and stagnation; the second is the period of transition, extending from the Conquest to the adoption of the charter of 1850; the third period ends with the adoption of the charter of 1851.

I.

The site of San Francisco was first trodden by Europeans in the autumn of 1769. At the same time, the bay of San Francisco was discovered. About three years later, in the spring of 1772, Pedro Fages and his followers looked out through the Golden Gate from the foot-hills of Berkeley. Towards the end of 1774, Bucareli, the viceroy of Mexico, wrote to Rivera and Serra that he intended to establish a presidio at San Francisco, and by an order dated November 12, 1775, he gave directions for the foundation of a fort, presidio, and mission on the bay of San Francisco. On the 12th of June, 1776, an overland expedition left Monterey to

5

carry out the order of the viceroy. It was composed of the lieutenant commanding, Don José Moraga, one sergeant, sixteen soldiers, seven settlers—all married men with their families—and a number of other persons, as servants, herdsmen, and drovers, who drove the two hundred head of neat cattle for the presidio, and the pack train with provisions and necessary equipage for the road.[1] They arrived on the 27th of June. The rest of the equipment was sent from Monterey by sea in the vessel "San Carlos," which arrived on the 18th of August. The site of the presidio having been determined, several rude buildings were erected. These were a storehouse, a chapel, the commandant's dwelling, and dwellings for the soldiers and their families. The ceremony of taking formal possession followed on the 17th of September. Father Palou, one of the two priests who had been sent with the expedition to establish a mission at San Francisco, thus records the event in which he was a principal actor: "We took formal possession of the presidio on the seventeenth day of September, the anniversary of the impressions of the wounds of our Father San Francisco, the patron of the presidio and mission. I said the first mass, and after blessing the site, the elevation and adoration of the Holy Cross, and the conclusion of the service with the *Te Deum*, the officers took formal possession in the name of our sovereign, with many discharges of cannon, both on sea and land, and the musketry of the soldiers."[2] The seventeenth of September, 1776, may therefore be set down as the date of the foundation of San Francisco. The ceremonies attending the foundation of the mission at San Francisco were held on the 9th of the following October.

From this beginning grew the town or pueblo of San Francisco, which, like the pueblo of San Diego, Santa Barbara, or Monterey, was an off-shoot of a presidio. It is to be dis-

---

[1] Palou, "Vida de Junipero serra," cap. **xlv**; also, Palou, "Noticias de la Nueva California," Parte Cuarta, cap. **xviii**.

[2] Palou, "Vida de Junipero Serra," cap. **xlv**.

tinguished from two other classes of pueblos, namely, those pueblos which were founded as such, and those which grew out of mission establishments. Vancouver has given a description of the presidio as it appeared in 1792, sixteen years after its foundation. " Its wall, which fronted the harbor, was visible from the ships; but instead of the city or town, whose lights we had so anxiously looked for on the night of our arrival, we were conducted into a spacious verdant plain, surrounded by hills on every side, excepting that which fronted the fort. The only object of human industry which presented itself was a square area, whose sides were about two hundred yards in length, inclosed by a mud wall, and resembling a pound for cattle. Above this wall the thatched roofs of their low, small houses just made their appearance. Their houses were all along the wall, within the square, and their fronts uniformly extended the same distance into the area, which is a clear, open space, without building, or other interruptions. The only entrance into it is by a large gateway; facing which, and against the center of the opposite wall or side, is the church; which, though small, was neat in comparison to the rest of the buildings. This projects further into the square than the houses, and is distinguishable from the other edifices by being white-washed with lime made from seashells; limestone or calcareous earth not having yet been discovered in the neighborhood. On the left of the church is the commandant's house, consisting, I believe, of two rooms and a closet, which are divided by massy walls, similar to that which incloses the square, and communicating with each other by very small doors. Between these apartments and the outward wall was an excellent poultry house and yard, which seemed pretty well stocked; and between the roof and the ceilings of the rooms was a kind of lumber garret: these were all the conveniences the habitation seemed calculated to afford. The rest of the houses, though smaller, were fashioned exactly after the same manner, and in the winter or rainy seasons must, at the best, be very uncomfortable dwellings. For, though the walls are a sufficient security against the inclemency of the weather, yet the windows, which are cut in the front wall, and look into the square, are destitute of glass, or any other defense that does not at the same time exclude the light.

" The apartment in the commandant's house into which we were ushered was about thirty feet long, fourteen feet broad, and twelve feet high; and the other room or chamber I judged to be of the same dimensions, excepting in its length, which appeared to be somewhat less. The floor was of the native soil, raised about three feet from its original level, without being boarded, paved, or even reduced to an even surface; the roof was covered with flags and rushes, the walls on the inside had once been white-washed; the furniture consisted of a very sparing assortment of the most indispensable articles, of the rudest fashion, and of the meanest kind, and ill accorded with the ideas one had conceived of the sumptuous manner in which the Spaniards live on this side of the globe."[1]

The presidio was directly under military rule, and represented the military element in Spanish colonization : while the pueblo and the mission represented the civil and religious elements respectively. In the beginning, the officers of the presidio of San Francisco were a lieutenant and a sergeant, assisted by a corporal or corporals.[2] Lieutenant José Moraga was commandant until his death, in 1785, and Pablo Grijalva was sergeant until 1787. In the presidial settlements of Spanish America we observe the carrying out of the Roman, rather than of the British, system of colonization. The main

---

[1] Vancouver, "A Voyage of Discovery to the North Pacific Ocean, and Round the World," III, 9–12; Hittell, I, 551, 583.

[2] De Mofras, writing of California between 1840 and 1842, sets down the annual cost of maintaining each presidio as about $55,000. Out of this a lieutenant is paid $550, a health officer, $450, an ensign, $400, a sergeant, $265, a corporal, $225, and seventy soldiers, $217 each. Each soldier had seven horses and a mule, kept on the king's farm. Artillery men were furnished from the marine department of San Blas. "Exploration de l'Oregon et des Californies," I, 287.

function of the presidio was to furnish military protection to the missions, and to such pueblos as were established within the limits of its jurisdiction, either as independent settlements, or as an outgrowth of the presidio itself. The abolition of the presidios as military posts was not thought of, because no time was foreseen when the country would no longer need an armed force.

The missions, on the other hand, were designed as temporary establishments. " It was contemplated," says Judge Felch, " that in ten years from their first foundation they should cease. It was supposed that within that period of time the Indians would be sufficiently instructed in Christianity and the arts of civilized life, to assume the position and character of citizens ; that these mission settlements would then become pueblos, and that the mission churches would become parish churches, organized like the other establishments of an ecclesiastical character, in other portions of the nation where no missions had ever existed. The whole missionary establishment was widely different from the ordinary ecclesiastical organizations of the nation. In it, the superintendence and charge was committed to priests, who were devoted to the special work of missions, and not to the ordinary clergy. The monks of the College of San Fernando and Zacatecas, in whose charge they were, were to be succeeded by the secular clergy of the National Church ; the missionary field was to become a diocese, the president of the missions to give place to a bishop, the mission churches to become curacies, and the faithful in the vicinity of each parish to become the parish worshippers."[1] " The Spanish government," says Hittell, " had from the very beginning contemplated secularization by finally transforming the missions into pueblos ; but the plan was based upon the idea of first educating the neophytes up to self-sustaining industry and citizenship."[2] The essentially

---

[1] Opinion in the California Board of Land Commissioners, in the case of the Bishop of California's petition for the churches.

[2] "History of California," I, 507.

temporary character of the missions rendered it impossible for them to acquire full ownership in the lands which they used. These lands " were occupied by them only by permission, but were the property of the nation, and at all times subject to grant under the colonization laws." [1]

The towns or pueblos, however, were looked upon as permanent institutions. The earliest towns of California were organized under the laws of Philip II., which specified two forms of settlements that might participate in the rights of a pueblo : 1, that made by a person under a contract with the government; 2, that made by a number of private persons acting under a mutual agreement among themselves. The conditions of the contract between the founder of the settlement and the government were : " That within the period of time which may be assigned to him, he must have at least thirty settlers, each one provided with a house, ten breeding cows, four oxen, or two oxen and two steers, one brood mare, one breeding sow, twenty breeding ewes of the Castilian breed, and six hens and one cock." The contractor was, moreover, required to appoint a priest to administer the holy sacrament, and to provide the church with ornaments, and things necessary for divine worship. After the first appointment, the church was to be subject to royal patronage. Failure on the part of the contractor to comply with his obligation, would subject him to a loss of whatever he had "constructed, wrought, or governed," which would be applied to the royal patrimony, and he would, furthermore, incur the penalty of one thousand pounds of gold ; but compliance with the terms of his obligation, would entitle him to four leagues of extent and territory in a square or prolonged form, according to the character of the land, in such manner that if surveyed there would be four leagues in a square. A final condition of this general grant was, that the limits of this territory should be distant at least five leagues from any

---

[1] Howard, U. S. S. C. Rep., p. 540.

city, town, or village of Spaniards previously founded, and that there should be no prejudice to any Indian town or private person.[1] Regarding the second form of settlement, the law provided that when at least ten married men should agree to form a new settlement, there would be given them the amount of land before specified, and also "power to elect among themselves alcaldes, with the usual jurisdiction, and annual officers of the council."[2] And "when a pueblo was once established, no matter how or by whom composed, and officially and legally recognized as such, it came immediately within the provisions of the general laws relating to pueblos, and was entitled to all the rights and privileges, whether political, municipal, or of property, which the laws conferred upon such organizations or corporations;"[3] and "among these rights was the right to four square leagues of land, in the form of a square, or in such other form as might be permitted by the nature of the situation."[4] The possession of this land, however, was not dependent on a "formal written grant."[5] The situation of San Francisco made it impossible for the town to obtain four square leagues in a square. Its territory was "bounded upon three sides by water, and the fourth line was drawn for quantity, east and west, straight across the peninsula, from the ocean to the bay. The four square leagues (exclusive of the military reserve, church buildings, etc.) north of this line, constitute the municipal lands of the pueblo of San Francisco,"[6]

After the secularization of the mission at San Francisco,

---

[1] "Recopilacion de Leyes de las Regnos de las Indias," Libro iv, Titulo v, Ley vi.

[2] "Recopilacion de Leyes de las Regnos de las Indias," Libro iv, Titulo v, Ley v.

[3] Hart *vs.* Burnett, Cal. Rep., 15, 541.

[4] Stevenson *vs.* Burnett, Cal. Rep., 35, 432.

[5] Hart *vs.* Burnett, Cal. Rep., 15, 542; Stevenson *vs.* Burnett, Cal. Rep., 35, 433.

[6] Payne & Dewey *vs.* Treadwell, Cal. Rep., 16, 230.

it was known sometimes as the "Pueblo de Dolores," but it had no separate municipal organization, and occupied the same legal position as some of the smaller "pueblos" of Mexico at the present time; it was embraced within a municipality of another name, to whose organization it was subordinated.[1]

⌠Many of the fundamental provisions regarding the local government of California under the old régime are derived immediately from the Spanish constitution of 1812, and a decree of the Spanish Cortes of the same year. These laws provided for town governments, composed of alcaldes, councilmen, and syndics, to be elected by a system of indirect election. Towns having less than one thousand inhabitants were required, on some holiday in the month of December, to elect nine electors; those having more than one thousand and less than five thousand, to elect sixteen; and those having more than five thousand inhabitants, to elect twenty-five electors. The constitution specifies with respect to this primary election, simply, that the citizens of the city or town shall assemble annually in the month of December, and elect a certain number of electors. But the Spanish Cortes of May 23, 1812, in order to avoid difficulties that might arise in a large town, or where the population subject to the government was scattered over an extensive area, decreed that each parish might constitute an electoral district, and elect the number of electors to which its proportion of the total population would entitle it. Where several small towns were united under a single government, no collection of less than fifty inhabitants would have the privilege of nominating an elector; but if the number of parishes happened to be greater than the number of electors to be appointed, still, in spite of all other provisions, each parish would be entitled to one elector. These provisions were made to apply not only to towns whose inhabitants were in the enjoyment of the

---

[1] "Derecho Politico de los Estados Unidos Mexicanos," II., 108.

rights of citizens, but also to those provincial towns whose
inhabitants, owing to peculiar circumstances, might not possess these rights.

The electors having been elected, either by parishes or by
the citizens, met in a common assembly; they were required
to meet on some other holiday in the month of December,
" to deliberate on the persons most suitable for the government of the town," and they were not allowed to adjourn
without having completed the election: the number of officers
to be elected varied with the populations of the towns. There
were required for each town not exceeding two hundred
inhabitants, one alcalde, two regidores or councilmen, and
one sindico procurador or prosecuting attorney ; for each
town having more than two hundred and less than five
hundred inhabitants, one alcalde, four regidores, and one
sindico ; for each town having between five hundred and
one thousand inhabitants, one alcalde, six regidores, and
one sindico ; for each town having between one thousand
and four thousand inhabitants, two alcaldes, eight regidores,
and two sindicos; and twelve regidores for each town of
more than four thousand inhabitants. In the capitals of the
provinces twelve regidores at least were required, and, in
case the town had more than ten thousand inhabitants, sixteen.

It was provided, moreover, that these officers should supersede all the municipal officers existing at the time of the
adoption of the Constitution. The term of office for the
alcaldes was one year; for the regidores or councilmen, two
years, one-half going out of office each year; for the syndicos,
one year, except in case there were two, when only one would
be replaced each year. Qualifications for any of these offices
were, that the person should be a citizen in the enjoyment of
his rights, twenty-five years old, and a resident of the place
for which he was elected for at least five years; also, that he
should hold no public office by appointment of the king.

The duties of these officers are indicated in the Constitution,
Articles 321–323, and are, in general, those which belong to

municipal governments everywhere. Under this Constitution, and the decree of the Spanish Cortes of May 23, 1812, there might be an ayuntamiento for a single town or pueblo, for a combination of several groups of inhabitants, each too small to have an ayuntamiento of its own, or for a pueblo to which were joined other such small groups of inhabitants. This law decreed by the Cortes survived the political revolution by which Mexico was severed from the mother country, and in many of its essential features it was continued as a law of Mexico till after California had fallen into the hands of the United States.

The Mexican Revolution of 1821 left the laws respecting private property within the ancient dominions of Spain in full force; and all titles to land that had been acquired before the revolution, whether by individuals, by a pueblo, or by any other corporation, remained valid under the Mexican republic. By the Mexican Colonization Laws of 1824 and 1828, such lands were expressly indicated as no longer within the field open to colonization.[1] Important changes, however, in the provisions for local government, were effected by the constitutional law of 1836, and the law of March 20, 1837, for the regulation of the interior government of the departments.[2] The Mexican Constitution of 1824 was a close copy of the Federal Constitution of the United States, and under it the several States enjoyed a large degree of independence. But in 1836 the political power of the nation became more thoroughly centralized, and the States and territories were reduced to departments, and made immediately subject to the supreme central government. Under this system Upper and Lower California became one department, which was divided into districts, and the districts into partidos. Over each district there was a prefect, and over each partido a subprefect; the former nominated by the governor of the department, and

---

[1] Dwinelle, "The Colonial History of the City of San Francisco," 41.
[2] Dublan y Lozano, "Legislacion Mexicana," III, 230, 258, 323.

confirmed by the general government, the latter nominated by the prefect and approved by the governor. In so far as the Constitution of 1836 varied from the Spanish Constitution of 1812, regarding town governments, the change was a restriction of local authority. It provided ayuntamientos only for capitals of departments, for places where they had existed in the year 1808, for seaports of four thousand and pueblos of eight thousand inhabitants: and besides the previously existing qualifications for office, there was required an annual income of at least five hundred dollars. The number of alcaldes, regidores, and syndicos had previously been fixed by law with reference to the number of the inhabitants; it was now left to the determination of the departmental councils with the concurrence of the governor; with, however, the provision that the first should not exceed six, the second, twelve, and the last, two. Vacancies, through death or inability to serve, were filled by a meeting of the electoral college called for that purpose; but vacancies which occurred within three months of the end of the year were filled at the annual election. If the ayuntamiento, or any part of it, were suspended, that of the preceding year, or the corresponding part of it, was required to act. Among those excluded from membership in the ayuntamiento were officers appointed by the congress, by the general government, or by the government of the department; the magistrates of the supreme tribunals of the departments; judges of first instance; ecclesiastics; persons in charge of hospitals, houses of refuge, or other establishments of public charity. These excluded classes, however, did not embrace appointees of the general or departmental government not domiciled in the place of official destination, nor retired soldiers resident in the territory of the respective ayuntamiento, and not supported exclusively by means of pensions.

Under these laws the ayuntamiento was subordinated to the sub-prefect of the partido in which its pueblo lay, and through the sub-prefect to the prefect of the district and to the governor of the department. Its functions were the care of the public health and accommodation, to watch over prisons, hospitals, and benevolent institutions that were not of private foundation, primary schools sustained by public funds, the construction and repair of bridges, highways, and roads, the raising and expenditure of public moneys from taxes, licenses, and the rents of municipal property; to promote the advancement of agriculture, industry, and commerce, and to assist the alcaldes in the preservation of peace and public order among the inhabitants.[1]

The alcaldes were required to maintain good order and public tranquillity; to watch over the execution and fulfilment of the police regulations, and of the laws, decrees, and orders communicated to them by the sub-prefects, or by the prefects in want of the sub-prefects; to ask from the military commanders the armed force which they might need, or to organize the citizens for their own defense; to secure the arrest and trial of the offenders; to see that the citizens subsist by useful occupations, and to reprehend idlers, vagrants, persons without any fixed place of abode, or any known employment; to impose executively a fine to the amount of twenty-five dollars on all disturbers of the peace, or to condemn them for four days to the public works, or to cause them to be arrested for double that period; governing themselves according to the circumstances of the individuals, and giving them a hearing summarily and verbally if they demanded it; but with respect to offenses which have a penalty affixed to them by law, the legal dispositions remaining in force were to be observed. The alcaldes, moreover, assisted and voted at the sessions of the ayuntamiento, and presided over them in the order of their appointment, when neither the prefect nor sub-prefect was present, the presiding alcalde deciding in the case of a tie vote. Temporary vacancies in the office of alcalde were filled by the regidores in the order of their election.[2]

---

[1] Constitution of 1836, Part VI, Art. 25.
[2] Law of March 20, 1837, Arts. 166–176.

The immediate government of towns deprived of ayuntamientos by the legislation of 1836 and 1837 was to be in the hands of justices of the peace, the number for each town being fixed by the departmental council, with the concurrence of the governor. They were to be appointed by the prefect of the district, on the recommendation of the respective subprefect. It was required that they should be Mexican citizens over twenty-five years of age, and residents of the towns for which they were appointed. In every place of at least a thousand inhabitants, the justices of the peace, in subjection to the sub-prefect, and through him to the superior authorities, had essentially the same powers and obligations as the ayuntamientos; and these justices of the peace, as well as those of places with less than a thousand inhabitants, had, moreover, the powers and obligations conferred by this law upon the alcaldes.[1]

Prior to 1834, there had been no ayuntamiento or common council at San Francisco. Captain Benjamin Morell, who visited the town in 1825, described it as "built in the same manner as Monterey, but much smaller, comprising only about one hundred and twenty houses and a church, with perhaps five hundred inhabitants." This estimate was probably largely in excess of the real number at that time;[2] for the census made in 1842 gives one hundred and ninety-six as the total population of the town at this date, seventeen years after Captain Morell's visit; and in June, 1847, it amounted to only four hundred and fifty-nine, three hundred and twenty-one of whom were males, and one hundred and thirty-eight females.

The government of this town or pueblo, before 1834, was in the hands of the territorial governor and the military commandant of the presidio. The former imposed license fees, and taxes, and the latter acted as a judge of first instance. Finally, in November of this year, the territorial governor,

---

[1] Law of March 20, 1837, Arts. 177-191.
[2] Dwinelle's "Colonial History," 41.

José Figueroa, wrote to the military commandant of San Francisco, stating that the territorial council had ordered the partido of San Francisco, which "embraced all Contra Costa, Sonoma, San Rafael, and, on this side of the bay, the whole of the present county of San Francisco,"[1] to proceed to the election of a constitutional ayuntamiento, which should reside in the presidio of that name, and be composed of an alcalde, two regidores, and a syndico, in accordance with the existing laws. It was ordered, moreover, that an account of the election should " be given by the proper way to the supreme government for the due approbation." By the same communication the commandant was informed that the ayuntamiento, when installed, would exercise the political functions with which he had been charged ; and the alcalde, the judicial functions which the laws, in lieu of a proper judge, had conferred upon him. The commandant was to be confined strictly to the functions of his military command.[2] It was proposed by this order to separate the military and civil power, and to bestow the latter upon a local organization. It was a "change of the former military government, which the commandant of the presidio had exercised, into a civil government for the same district."[3] This local government was what has been called an ayuntamiento aggregate, and was formed "for the purpose of giving a municipal government to those small populations of the partido which would not otherwise have an ayuntamiento."[4] It embraced under its jurisdiction, as already suggested, not only the inhabitants of the peninsula, but also those of the other side of the bay.[5]

---

[1] "Documents, Depositions, and Brief of Law Points raised thereon on behalf of the United States, before the U. S. Board of Land Commissioners." San Francisco, 1854, p. 67.

[2] Figueroa to the Military Commandant of San Francisco, Monterey, November 4, 1834. See Dwinelle, Addenda, No. xxi.

[3] "Documents, Depositions, and Brief," p. 67.

[4] Dwinelle's "Colonial History," 48.

[5] Governor José Figueroa wrote from Monterey, January 31, 1835, to the alcalde of San Francisco, as follows: "The appointment you have

As to the significance of this change, the opinion of the majority of the United States Land Commission for California is unequivocal: "After a careful examination of the whole testimony on this point, and the law applicable to the subject, we are brought to the conclusion that the effect of the proceedings of the territorial authorities in 1834, as shown by the official records and documents for the establishment of the ayuntamiento at the presidio of San Francisco, and the subsequent organization of that body in conformity therewith, was to erect the presidio into a pueblo or town, with all the civil and territorial rights which attached to such corporations under the Mexican laws then in force." [1]

The meeting for the election of electors, the *junta primaria*, was held on the first Sunday in December, 1834. On the third Sunday of the same month the electors chose the members of the ayuntamiento, which was installed January 1, 1835. The election was held at the house of the commandant of the presidio, and the voters came from the several places already indicated as embraced within the jurisdiction of the partido. Their eagerness to participate in the election is explained by their anxiety to get rid of the military authority. After the organization of the ayuntamiento, the records or archives were kept in a desk in one of the rooms at the presidio, where the meetings were held. But the place of meeting, whether at the presidio, the mission, or the village of Yerba Buena, is not a matter of importance, since all were within the limits of a common jurisdiction.

Not long after this organization of the partido was effected, the government concluded, from a census of the town, that, under the law of May 23, 1812, which was still considered to be in force, San Francisco itself was entitled to an ayunta-

---

made in favor of the citizen Gregorio Briones, as auxiliary alcalde in Contra Costa, seems to be very well, and consequently has my approval. I say this to you in answer to your official note on the matter, of the 22d ultimo."
[1] City of San Francisco *vs.* The United States.

miento, and therefore ordered the commandant to cause to be elected one alcalde, two regidores, and one syndico; in other words, the officers prescribed by law for towns of more than fifty, and less than two hundred inhabitants. The census which was the basis of this conclusion probably included not only the population at the Presidio[1] and the Mission, but also that at other points on the northern part of the peninsula. San Francisco appears not to have been specifically the Presidio, the Mission, or Yerba Buena, but to have comprehended them all; for during seven years after the establishment of the government of San Francisco, the offices of this government were at different times indifferently at the Presidio, at the Mission, and at Yerba Buena, and still it remained throughout the government of San Francisco.

In accordance with the governor's order, addressed to the commandant, a primary election of nine electors was held December 13, 1835. This election, like the first, was held at the house of the commandant. On the 27th of the same month, the electors met for the purpose of electing one alcalde and the other officers; and thus was constituted the first ayuntamiento of the pueblo of San Francisco, which superseded the ayuntamiento of the partido. Of this government, Dwinelle says: "Instead of being an aggregated ayuntamiento, composed of small populations in the *partido*, it was an ayuntamiento of the *pueblo*, to which various small populations of the partido were aggregated;"[2] or, as he has elsewhere styled it, a composite ayuntamiento. The town government thus established was endowed with those powers which, under the Spanish laws of 1812, belonged to the fully organized

---

[1] According to Francisco Sanchez, who was the commandant at the Presidio in 1838, the only persons residing here at this time were Candelario Miranda, Joaquin Pina, and Eusebio Soto. Pina was a corporal of artillery, and Soto was a private. Antonio Soto and Apolonario Miranda lived on lots near the Presidio, at the left of the road going from Yerba Buena to the Presidio.

[2] "Col. Hist.," 51.

pueblo, and it was continued in existence by virtue of these laws.

When, however, the Constitution of 1836 came into operation in California, it led to important changes in municipal affairs. Except capitals of departments and places which were regarded as pueblos before 1808, no town of less than four thousand inhabitants was permitted to have an ayuntamiento. Under this law, the government which had been set up at San Francisco in 1835 was abolished. The ayuntamiento elected January 8, 1838, appears to have been the last one constituted in this town before the Constitution of 1836, as supplemented by the law of March 20, 1837, came into full operation. In his message of February 16, 1840, the governor announced that "there is no ayuntamiento whatever in the department; for, there being no competent number of inhabitants in any of the towns, as provided by the constitution, those then existing had to be dissolved; and only in the capital there ought to be one of such bodies."[1] Having, then, documentary evidence of the election of an ayuntamiento, on January 8, 1838, and the statement of the governor that no ayuntamiento existed here in February, 1840, it is clear that it must have ceased to exist at some point between these two dates. The government then passed into the hands of justices of the peace, who were provided, in towns of less than four thousand inhabitants, with the powers and functions of alcaldes and ayuntamientos.

It is not to be supposed that the people of San Francisco, in electing an ayuntamiento, in January, 1838, were acting in conscious violation of a law which deprived them of this privilege. Their action is rather to be explained by the fact that, although the constitution was promulgated at the end of 1836, and the supplementary law regarding the internal government of the departments was passed the following March, no information of these events had reached San Francisco

---

[1] Dwinelle, "Col. Hist.," Addenda, No. I, p. 70.

prior to the date of this last election. That delay like this was not unusual, may be seen from the fact that certain election laws, passed by the supreme government November 30, 1836, were not received and proclaimed in California till January, 1839, and also from the statement of De Mofras, that "official despatches were often a year in the passage between California and Mexico."[1]

Although San Francisco was, at this time, deprived of its council, it did not relinquish its character as a pueblo. "Accordingly, we find that when the pueblo of San Francisco, after the American conquest of California, attained the requisite population, it again elected its ayuntamiento, not under any provisions of the laws of the conquerors, but under these very provisions of the Mexican constitution of 1836, under which the ayuntamiento of the pueblo was suspended in 1839."[2]

In 1839, San Francisco had been founded more than sixty years; still it was without a jail, from which it is to be inferred that but little progress had been made in civilization. Finding the criminal Galindo on their hands, the inhabitants of San Francisco, through Justice De Haro, asked of the governor that he might be sent to San José, which was already provided with a prison. Besides the lack of a jail, another reason for the request was that the inhabitants of the place were scattered, each having his agricultural and stock interests at a great distance from the town, so that there were very few remaining to guard the criminal, and these could not spare the time from their personal business.

The law under which the governmental power of San Francisco was transferred to justices of the peace, made no provision in towns not entitled to have ayuntamientos for a syndico, or an officer known as sindico procurador; yet, on July 20, 1839, Francisco Guerrero, justice of the peace at San

---

[1] Vol. I, p. 222. See Hittell, I, 542.
[2] Dwinelle, "Col. Hist.," 64.

Francisco, proposed to the prefect of the first district to appoint Don Juan Fuller as a sindico procurador for this place, "for the better management of the municipal rents." Fuller appears to have been appointed, for there exists an account made out by Don Juan Fuller as sindico of the municipality of San Francisco, embracing the period between August, 1839, and January, 1842. This office was continued to the last year of Mexican dominion. In order to relieve the justices of the peace, and to enable them to devote themselves to the duties peculiar to their office, Governor Micheltorena, on November 14, 1843, ordered the election of two alcaldes in San Francisco, and in each of several other towns of the department. By this order it was required that the election should be indirect; that seven electors should be chosen on the second Sunday of December, who should meet on the following Friday to elect the alcaldes. The newly elected officers were required to go into office on the 1st day of January, 1844, the first alcaldes to perform the duties of judges of first instance, and to take charge of the prefectures of the respective districts. The first alcalde appointed by this election was Guillermo Hinckley. The election of the following December resulted in the appointment of Juan N. Padilla, who took the customary oath, and entered upon the duties of his office January 1, 1845. On July 7, 1846, that portion of California which embraces San Francisco passed under the dominion of the United States.

Foreseeing the outbreak of hostilities between Mexico and the United States, George Bancroft, Secretary of the Navy, under date of June 24, 1845, sent a secret and confidential communication to Commodore John D. Sloat, then in command of the United States naval forces in the Pacific, and called his attention particularly to the existing relations between this country and Mexico. "It is the earnest desire of the President," he wrote, "to pursue the policy of peace; and he is anxious that you, and every part of your squadron, should be assiduously careful to avoid any act which could be construed as an act of aggression. Should Mexico, however, be resolutely bent on hostilities, you will be mindful to protect the persons and interests of citizens of the United States near your station ; and should you ascertain, beyond a doubt, that the Mexican government has declared war against us, you will at once employ the force under your command to the best advantage. The Mexican ports on the Pacific are said to be open and defenseless. If you ascertain with certainty that Mexico has declared war against the United States, you will at once possess yourself of the port of San Francisco, and blockade or occupy such other ports as your force may permit. Yet, even if you should find yourself called upon, by the certainty of an express declaration of war against the United States, to occupy San Francisco and other Mexican ports, you will be careful to preserve, if possible, the most friendly relations with the inhabitants, and where you can do so, you will encourage them to adopt a course of neutrality." In a subsequent order to Commodore Sloat, issued after the beginning of hostilities, the Secretary wrote : "You will consider the most important object to be, to take and to hold possession of San Francisco ; and this you will do without fail."[1] The occasion for acting under these orders came in 1846. Having received at Mazatlan the information that the Mexican troops had, by order of the Mexican government, invaded the territory of the United States, and attacked the forces under General Taylor, Commodore Sloat sailed on the 8th of June, in the "Savannah," for the coast of California, to execute the order of June 24, 1845. They arrived at Monterey July 2, 1846, and on the 7th of the same month took possession of the town, raised the standard of the Union, and issued to the inhabitants of California a proclamation announcing the designs of the government of the United States, at the same time pointing out the grounds of hope for the people under the new rule. In order that the

---

[1] Geo. Bancroft to Com. John D. Sloat, May 15, 1846.

public tranquillity might not be disturbed, the judges, alcaldes and other civil officers were invited to execute their functions as heretofore; at least, until more definite arrangements could be made for the government of the territory. Assurance was, moreover, given that "all persons holding titles to real estate, or in quiet possession of land under color of right," should have those titles guaranteed to them; and that "all churches and the property they contain, in possession of the clergy of California," should continue in their existing rights and possessions.

In the meantime, the "Portsmouth" was at San Francisco awaiting orders, which were received by Commodore Montgomery on the evening of July 8. At 7 o'clock the following morning, he hoisted the American flag at San Francisco, issued Commodore Sloat's proclamation, and took possession of the region in the name of the United States.

The result of these events, when confirmed by the peace between Mexico and the United States, was to transfer the sovereign power over this region from the Mexican government to the government of the United States; but the existing laws and machinery of local government were temporarily maintained, and Lieutenant Washington A. Bartlett was appointed by Montgomery as the first alcalde of San Francisco under the new regime.

II.

The law of 1836, by which San Francisco was deprived of its ayuntamiento in 1839, left the governmental power of the municipality in the hands of justices of the peace. But when California passed under the dominion of the United States, the most important officer in the municipal government of San Francisco was the alcalde. This change had been effected by the order of Governor Micheltorena, in 1843, acting "with the extraordinary powers conferred on him by the President under the Basis of Tacubaya." [1]   Monterey and Los Angeles were required to elect ayuntamientos, each composed of two alcaldes, four regidores, and one sindico. The other towns were required to elect "two alcaldes of first and second nomination." "They were to enter upon their duties the first of the following January, and in addition to the judicial powers of the ordinary alcaldes and the political powers of the prefects, they were to exercise the powers and obligations which the ayuntamientos have." [2]

Under the Méxican régime alcaldes possessed the powers and jurisdiction of judges of first instance, and it is believed that no other judges of first instance were appointed or held office in California at this time. [3]   The alcaldes, to a great extent, both made and enforced the law ; "at least, they paid but little regard either to American or Mexican law further than suited their own convenience, and conduced to their own profit." [4]   The alcalde, as well as the justice of the peace, usually exercised judicial, but sometimes political, functions. [5] His judicial functions were relatively prominent when his office existed in union with an ayuntamiento. The writers of the "Annals of San Francisco," speaking evidently from the experience of their own city, assign to the alcalde the entire

---

[1] Cal. Rep., iii, 449.

[2] Cal. Rep., 15, 558.

[3] "By the articles 26, 27, and 28 of a decree made on the second day of March, 1843, alcaldes and justices of the peace in the departments of California, New Mexico, and Tabasco, were empowered to perform the functions of Judges of First Instance in those districts in which there were no judges of first instance." "There was no Judge of First Instance in the district of San Francisco." Cal. Rep., i, 220, 508.

[4] Cal. Rep., i, Pref. vii.

[5] Dwinelle, v. Bondelier, in his "Tour in Mexico," speaks of a military function which the alcalde also exercised: "Still there existed, as late as 1587, a war-captain (capitan de la guerra) of Cholula. That officer was at the same time Alcalde (Justice). It is probable that, under the influence of two centuries of constant peace, the latter office prevailed, and the war-captain completely disappears." p. 154.

control of the municipal affairs, and an administration of justice "pretty much according to his own ideas of the subject; without being tied down to precedents and formal principles of law."[1] A contemporary account of the functions of the alcalde, published in *The California Star*, April 17, 1847, agrees essentially with the foregoing. "There being no law defining the powers and duties of the alcaldes, it is impossible for them to know of what subjects they have cognizance, or over what extent of country they have jurisdiction. By some, who pretend to be well versed in the invisible laws of California, it is insisted that the jurisdiction of the alcaldes extends to no matters of difference where the amount in controversy exceeds one hundred dollars, and that each is confined to his particular district, in his judicial acts. Others urge, that as to amount their jurisdiction is unlimited, and that the alcaldes who resided at the principal towns, have both appellate and original jurisdiction throughout the entire department in which they reside." A specific limitation, however, was set to the alcalde's power by Mason's circular, dated at Monterey, August 23, 1847. By this the alcalde was forbidden to perform the marriage ceremony where either of the parties was a member of the Catholic Church in California, the object of this limitation being "to secure to the Californians the full enjoyment of their religion and religious privileges." But in spite of such limitations, there remained abundant ground of dissatisfaction. The grievances frequently found expression in *The California Star*. "When California was taken possession of," it was said editorially on June 19, 1847, "it was the duty of our rulers to have continued in existence the laws of Mexico; this was proclaimed

---

[1] "The Annals of San Francisco." By Frank Soulé, John H. Gihon, and James Nisbet. 179. In a conversation between Wilkes and Don Pedro, alcalde of San José, Wilkes asked the alcalde "by which law he administered justice; his answer was—by what he thought right." Wilkes, "Expedition," v. 208.

by Commodore Stockton, but never put in operation. For example, one of the laws of the Republic is, that there shall be an alcalde's court established in each particular neighborhood, a district court in each of the three districts, to which appeals may be taken from the alcaldes, and a court of appeals at Monterey, to which appeals may be taken from the district courts. This law has, been annulled, and instead of this organization, we have alcaldes all over the country, who claim original and ultimate jurisdiction over all matters of difference between citizens, of whatever amount, and if either party feels dissatisfied with their decisions, he goes in person to the governor, makes an *ex parte* statement of the case, and obtains a stay of proceedings, or reversal of the judgment, as the will of the military commandant may dictate. Or, if a culprit be sentenced to hard labor, or imprisonment, and is sent to Monterey for punishment, to the Rev. Puissant-Coke, alcalde of that renowned burg, he dismisses him to the field of his former crimes, with the godly admonition, ' Go, and sin no more.' The thief pays his fee and re-enters upon the duties of his profession."

Under Spanish and Mexican laws, it was provided that the alcalde, in all cases of a civil nature, which might be terminated by an agreement of the parties, should " require conciliatory measures to be tried until they should result either in a satisfactory arrangement or in the entire failure to accomplish a reconciliation."[1] One of the alcalde's most important functions is, therefore, to act as mediator between parties in dispute. Cases which may come under the jurisdiction of the judge of the district shall be presented to the competent alcalde, who, with two good men, one nominated by each party, shall hear them both, take account of their affirmations, and, having heard the opinions of the two associates, shall within eight days at the most announce the terms of conciliation which appear to him proper to terminate the

---

[1] Cal. Rep., i, 60, 61.

litigation without further progress. If the parties acquiesce in this judgment, the case is thereby ended, and the result is noted in a book.

The four years between the appointment of Lieutenant Bartlett to be the first alcalde of San Francisco, under the authority of the United States, and the adoption of the first charter under the constitution of California, constitute a period of transition, a period in which the city was seeking a foundation for its government. Mr. Bartlett held the office of alcalde from July 9, 1846, to February 22, 1847, but during about a month of this time, subsequent to the 20th of December, he was a prisoner in the hands of the Mexican Californians; and during his absence George Hyde, by the appointment of Captain J. B. Hull, performed the duties of the office. Mr. Bartlett resigned in order to return to his naval duties, and after his resignation General Kearney appointed Edwin Bryant as his successor.

A short time before he resigned, Mr. Bartlett was publicly charged by C. E. Pickett with misappropriating funds belonging to the town. In reply to this charge, he demanded of Capt. J. B. Hull, then commanding the Northern District of California, that a commission of inquiry should examine into the state of the accounts of his office.[1] In accordance with this request, Captain Hull appointed W. D. M. Howard, William A. Leidesdorff, and Francisco Guerrero a committee to make the investigation, " with a view to ascertain, whether any of the funds of the office have been applied to any object, other than the proper expenses belonging to it, and if so, what amount, and by whose authority, and also, whether there is a deficiency in the funds, not properly accounted for."[2] The result of this examination was embodied in the com-

---

[1] Washington A. Bartlett to Joseph B. Hull, July 12, 1847. See *The California Star*, January 23, 1847.

[2] Joseph B. Hull to Howard, Leidesdorff, and Guerrero, January 15, 1847. See *The California Star*, January 23, 1847.

mittee's report completely exonerating the alcalde from the charge of misapplying the funds of his office. Mr. Bartlett was, therefore, directed by Captain Hull to resume the duties of alcalde, which in the meantime had been performed by Mr. Hyde.[1] The report of this commission is also important as showing the actual receipts of the municipal funds from the 15th of August to the 11th of December, 1846, which amounted to five hundred dollars and twenty-five cents ($500.25), besides a port fund of two hundred and forty-six dollars and seventy-five cents ($246.75). The principal source of this revenue was the business transacted in the alcalde's office. Another source was an annual license fee of ten dollars for the sale of liquors, and a small amount was also "received on account of lots unoccupied or taken up in Yerba Buena."[2]

Mr. Bryant remained in office only till the first of June, 1847, when he resigned; but he appears to have remained long enough to gain the good opinion of his fellow-citizens. George Hyde was appointed by General Kearney to succeed Mr. Bryant. During his period of office, Mr. Hyde found that the business of the local government had increased to such an extent that its proper management was beyond his unaided ability; he therefore, on the 28th of July, selected six gentlemen to assist him. These were William A. Leidesdorff, Robert A. Parker, José P. Thompson, Pedro T. Sherreback, John Rose, and Benjamin R. Buckalew. They were called the ayuntamiento, or town council, although not constituted in the manner provided by law for establishing that body. They were to remain in office until superseded by members elected under an order by the governor. An ordinance providing for such an election was issued by Governor

---

[1] J. B. Hull to W. A. Bartlett, January 18, 1847. See *The California Star*, January 23, 1847.

[2] The report was dated January 16, 1847, and was printed in *The California Star*, January 30, 1847.

Mason on the 15th of August. It cites the need of a more efficient government, and indicates the principal features of that about to be established. "There is wanted," he says, "in San Francisco[1] an efficient town government, more so than is in the power of an alcalde to put in force. There may be soon expected a large number of whalers in your bay, and a large increase of your population by the arrival of immigrants. It is therefore highly necessary that you should at an early day have an efficient town police, proper town laws, town officers, etc., for enforcement of the laws, for the preservation of order, and for the proper protection of persons and property.

"I therefore desire that you call a town meeting for the election of six persons, who, when elected, shall constitute the town council, and who, in conjunction with the alcalde, shall constitute the town authorities until the end of the year 1848.

"All the municipal laws and regulations will be framed by the council, but executed by the alcalde in his judicial capacity as at present.

"The first alcalde will preside at all meetings of the council, but shall have no vote, except in cases where the votes are equally divided.

"The town council (not less than four of whom shall constitute a quorum for the transaction of business) shall appoint all the town officers, such as treasurer, constables, watchmen, etc., and determine their pay, fees, etc.

"The treasurer shall enter into ample and sufficient bonds, conditioned for the faithful performance of his duties; the bonds to be fully executed to the satisfaction of the council before the treasurer enters upon his duties.

"The second alcalde shall, in case of the absence of the first alcalde, take his place and preside at the council, and there perform all the proper functions of the first alcalde.

---

[1] This name supersedes that of Yerba Buena in accordance with Bartlett's order of March, 1847.

" No soldier, sailor or marine, nor any person who is not a *bonâ fide* resident of the town shall be allowed to vote for a member of the town council."

Under this order, the alcalde, Mr. Hyde gave notice on the 30th of August, 1847, that there would be an election for six members of a town council for San Francisco, and that this election would be held at the alcalde's office on Monday, the 13th of September. In this notice it was ordered that the polls should be open from 12 to 2 o'clock, but later the time was extended so that the polls might remain open from 10 A. M. to 4 P. M. According to the governor's order, voting was to be confined to "*bonâ fide* residents of the town "; but it was found to be somewhat difficult to determine the exact limits of this definition. Of the population of the town at the time there exists no accurate account. In June, however, it was set down at four hundred and fifty-nine, of whom three hundred and twenty-one were males, and one hundred and thirty-eight females. But more than one hundred of the males were under twenty-one years of age, leaving somewhat over two hundred persons entitled by age and sex to vote. When the vote had been taken, it was found that precisely two hundred ballots had been cast for more than thirty different candidates. There appears to have been no efficient system of nomination, and in counting the vote the six persons who had received the highest numbers were declared elected. These were: William Glover, with 126 votes; W. D. M. Howard, with 114 votes; W. A. Leidesdorff, with 109 votes; E. P. Jones, with 88 votes; Robt. A. Parker, with 74 votes; and W. S. Clark, with 72 votes.

At the first meeting of this council, held September 16, 1847, W. A. Leidesdorff was elected town treasurer, and it was agreed that the clerk of the alcalde's office should act as secretary of the council, and for his services receive a suitable compensation. Messrs. Howard, Jones, and Clark were constituted a committee "to form a code of laws for the regulation of the affairs of the town." The result of their work was presented at the next meeting, held September 21, in the form of a body of rules for the government of the council. These rules being adopted, provided that the regular meetings of the council should be held on Monday evening, at seven o'clock, of each week until a different time should be agreed upon by a majority of all the members. Every motion, resolution, or other proposition was required to be put in writing and distinctly read, before any discussion on it would be allowed. After sufficient deliberation, the vote should be taken by the alcalde *viva voce.* The alcalde should decide all questions of order, from whose decision an appeal might be taken to the members present, in which case a majority deciding against the alcalde, his decision should be reversed. The alcalde's connection with the council was merely that of a presiding officer empowered to give "a casting vote in case of a tie." He could "not participate in the discussion of any subject, or give an opinion thereon." Any two members might call a meeting of the council at any time, provided that at least twelve hours previous notice were given by the secretary in writing.

At this meeting there was also adopted an ordinance making each member of the council a "conservator of the peace within the limits of the town." He might issue any process necessary to preserve the peace and morals of the place, upon application or when he might deem it proper to do so. Such process was ` made returnable to the alcalde, and was to "be charged and regarded by the alcalde as if it had been issued by himself."

Not long after its organization, the council resolved itself into a "committee of the whole to wait upon the governor to learn his views upon the duties of the council."[1] In reply to this request, Governor Mason wrote "that the jurisdiction of the present town council of San Francisco is confined to the limits of the town survey, the boundaries of which I have instructed the alcalde to have marked as soon as convenient."

---

[1] *The Californian,* September 29, 1847.

On a second point, he informs them that the duties of the council were prospective, not retrospective, that they could "not impair the obligation of contracts entered into by the previous town authorities, nor take jurisdiction of the actions or conduct of such authorities, further than to modify or repeal any law or ordinance created by the previous government and now in force which they might deem inconsistent with the interest of the community."[1] In this communication the governor strongly recommended that whatever expenses might be contemplated, "the town be kept perfectly free of debt."

Mr. Hyde had never been a popular magistrate. Frequent charges against him found their way to the public, and the governor had been several times petitioned to remove him. Finally, in this letter to the council, he authorizes that body to make a thorough investigation of these charges, and report to him the facts, together with their opinion. This action of the governor gave general satisfaction, but of the nine charges made against the alcalde, the investigation resulted in establishing only two, and these were not deemed by the governor adequate ground for removal from office. But the indignant populace demanded their victim, and Mr. Hyde saw fit to resign April 3, 1848. During the administration of Mr. Hyde Governor Mason had appointed T. M. Leavenworth to the office of second alcalde of San Francisco, and now on the resignation of the first alcalde, Mr. John Townsend was appointed to fill the vacancy.

By an ordinance passed September 28, 1847, the chief police force of the town was made to consist of two elected constables, who should "perform all duties required of other ministerial officers within the town, who should faithfully execute all processes directed to them in accordance with law, and make due returns thereof," and who should "strictly enforce and obey every law, ordinance and resolution passed by the coun-

---

[1] R. B. Mason to the Town Council, Elect. of San Francisco, October 1, 1847. See *The Californian*, October 6, 1847.

cil." The constables were to "receive for the service of any writ or other process, one dollar, to be paid out of the fines imposed upon cases, one dollar for the service of any writ or other process, to be paid by the defeated party, also ten cents per mile for every mile which they might travel to serve any writ or other process beyond the limits of the town."[1]

While San Francisco was thus making progress towards a well-ordered local government, it was suddenly stricken as with a plague.[2] On the 19th of January, 1848, gold was discovered on the north fork of the American river. It required several weeks to spread the news of the discovery, and still longer to convince the unsuspecting inhabitants that a vast treasure had been revealed. But when the real significance of the revelation dawned on the public mind, it produced a wild frenzy of desire to participate in the harvest of gold. San Francisco, which had already become the leading town of the territory, was a scene of sudden desolation. Its houses were left unoccupied and unprotected; its former trade ceased; its lots fell to a small part of their earlier value; its two newspapers, *The Californian* and *The California Star*,[3] were suspended in May and June; and the town, deserted by the bulk of its inhabitants, was at one time without a single officer clothed with civil authority. It is asserted, moreover, that at one time only five men were left in the town. But when the news had spread to the other side of the country, and to other lands, and the Argonauts began to find their way through the Golden Gate, the opportunities of trade at San Francisco brought the town once more into active existence.

In the beginning of October, 1848, the town had so far revived as to be able to hold an election. Dr. T. M. Leaven-

---

[1] See *The Californian*, October 6, 1847.

[2] "Master and man alike hurried to the *placeres*, leaving San Francisco, like a place where the plague reigns, forsaken by its old inhabitants, a melancholy solitude." Annals, 204.

[3] *The Californian* was suspended May 29, 1848, and *The California Star* June 14, 1848. *The Californian* was revived on the 15th of July.

worth was a second time chosen first alcalde, and B. R. Buckalew and Barton Mowrey were elected town councillors. At this election one hundred and fifty-eight votes were polled. On the 9th of October, the town council met for the first time since May, and adjourned to the 11th, when the limits of the town for the administration of justice were defined. The boundary as given in the resolution was: " That the line shall commence at the mouth of Creek Guadalupe, where it empties into the Bay of San Francisco, following the course of said stream to its head waters; from thence a due west line to the Pacific Ocean; thence northwards along the coast to the inlet to the harbor of the bay; thence eastwardly, through the middle of the said inlet into the Bay of San Francisco, and embracing the entire anchorage ground from the inlet to the mouth of the Creek Guadalupe." [1]

In accordance with Mason's order the first elected town council was to remain in power until the end of the year 1848. On the 27th of December, the town council for 1849 was elected, the number of votes cast being three hundred and forty-seven. The members elected were Stephen C. Harris, W. D. M. Howard, George C. Hubbard, Robert A. Parker, Thomas J. Roach, John Sirrine, and John Townsend. The old town council of 1848 was opposed to the continuance of the new one, because a certain number of unqualified persons had voted at the election, and therefore ordered a new election. On the 15th of January, 1849, another town council was consequently elected, composed of Stephen C. Harris, Lazarus Everhart, Stephen A. Wright, Daniel Storks, Isaac Montgomery, John Sirrine, and C. E. Wetmore, two of the members being common to this and the council elected in December. There were thus three town councils claiming an authoritative existence. That elected in December denied entirely the right of the old council to further power, while that in turn acknowledged the town

---

[1] "Annals," 207.

council elected in January, and proposed to transfer to it the municipal records.

The confusion which was here manifest in the local affairs of San Francisco, was only an index of the attitude into which the inhabitants of California had everywhere fallen. They appeared to be without any recognized political status. They believed that they could not safely wait for Congress to give them a government, and therefore determined to form one for themselves. "Accordingly, attempts were soon severally made by the people of San Francisco, Sonoma, and Sacramento, to form legislatures for themselves, which they invested with supreme authority. Other portions of the country prepared to follow the example of the places named."[1] At San Francisco, in answer to a previous call, the citizens of the town and district held a meeting in the public square, February 12, 1849.[2] Myron Norton presided, and T. W. Perkins acted as secretary. The object of the meeting having been stated by the chairman, Mr. Hyde introduced a plan of organization or government for the district of San Francisco, which grew out of the "necessity of having some better defined and more permanent civil regulations for our general security than the vague, unlimited, and irresponsible authority" which then existed. It provided for a legislative assembly for the district of San Francisco, consisting of fifteen members, citizens of the district, eight of whom should constitute a quorum for the transaction of business. The assembly was empowered to make such laws as it might deem essential to promote the happiness of the people, provided they should not conflict with

---

[1] Annals, 135.

[2] The confusion was greatly increased by the incoming tide of population. Between January 1 and June 30, 1849, 15,000 persons are said to have been added to the population of the country, 10,000 of whom came by sea and landed at San Francisco. There were among these only 200 females. The second half of the year the arrivals averaged 4,000 a month, and only 500 females in the whole 24,000. At the close of 1849 the population of San Francisco was between 20,000 and 25,000.

the Constitution of the United States, nor be repugnant to the common law. To become a law a bill had to be passed by the legislative assembly and to be signed by the speaker and the recording clerk. It was required, moreover, that the legislative assembly should determine its own rules, and keep a journal of its proceedings, and that the members should enter upon the duties of their office on the first Monday of March.

In addition to the legislative assembly, the plan proposed by Mr. Hyde provided that for the purpose of securing to the people a more efficient administration of law and justice, there should be elected by ballot three justices of the peace, of equal though separate jurisdiction, who should be empowered by their commission of office to hear and adjudicate all civil and criminal issues in the district, according to the common law; that an election of members of the legislative assembly and of justices of the peace should be held on Wednesday, February 21, 1849; and that all should hold office "for the term of one year from the date of their commissions, unless sooner superseded by the competent authorities from the United States government, or by the action of a provisional government now invoked by the people of this territory, or by the action of the people of this district." In the several articles as well as in the oath to be required of officers, the supremacy of the Federal government was fully recognized. [1]

Considering the importance of the matters in hand, the action of the meeting appears startlingly sudden. It is difficult to find a briefer history of the establishment of a government than that contained in the records of this meeting. "Mr. Harris moved the adoption of the plan entire," so runs the record, "which was seconded; when Mr. Buckalew moved to supersede the plan of government presented, by submitting the subject to a committee to be appointed by the meeting, and whose duty it should be to report to an adjourned meet-

---

[1] Executive Document No. 17, House of Rep., 1st Session, 31st Congress, p. 728.

ing. Thereupon an animated discussion ensued. Mr. Buckalew's motion having been seconded, was lost by vote; when the question recurred on the original motion of Mr. Harris, which was carried almost unanimously."[1] By further action of the meeting, it was determined that every male resident of the age of twenty-one years or upwards, should be entitled to vote, and that the members of the town councils claiming authority should be requested to resign, and a committee was appointed to receive their resignations.

In accordance with the provisions of this fundamental law, an election was held on the 21st of February, when Myron Norton, Heron R. Per Lee, and William M. Stewart were elected justices of the peace. The members of the legislative assembly elected at the same time were Stephen A. Wright, Alfred J. Ellis, Henry A. Harrison, George C. Hubbard, George Hyde, Isaac Montgomery, William M. Smith, Andrew J. Grayson, James Creighton, Robert A. Parker, Thomas J. Roach, William F. Swasey, Talbot H. Green, Francis J. Lippitt, and George Hawk Lemon. They took the prescribed oath, which was administered by Justice Per Lee, and held their first meeting on the evening of March 5. At this meeting the legislative assembly elected Francis J. Lippitt speaker and J. Howard Ackerman clerk. In the second and third meetings, it completed its organization by adopting rules for conducting business, and by appointing a list of standing committees.

These rules embodied the ordinary provisions for conducting business in a parliamentary assembly. The speaker had no vote, except in cases of tie, and in cases of ballot. Special meetings might be called at any time by the speaker on the written application of three members. Every petition or other paper presented to the assembly was referred to its appropriate standing committee as a matter of course, without a vote, unless such reference was objected to by some member.

---

[1] Dwinelle, "Colonial History."

All resolutions and reports of committees were required to lie on the table for consideration till the next meeting. Bills were introduced either on the report of a committee or by motion for leave, and in the latter case a day's notice of the motion was required. Before becoming a law a bill was required to be read three times, and after the second reading it could not be amended by the assembly, except on the recommendation of a committee to which at any stage of its progress it might be committed. The enacting clause was in these words: " The people of the district of San Francisco, California, represented in Assembly, do enact as follows:" Having passed the assembly a bill required the signatures of the speaker and of the recording clerk before it could obtain the validity of a law.

There were five standing committees provided for: a committee on ways and means; a committee on the judiciary; a committee on expenditure; a committee on public health and police; a committee on public buildings and improvements. These committees were appointed by ballot, one vote being taken for the chairman of each committee, and one vote for the other members in a body. All other committees were appointed by acclamation and a plurality of votes was necessary for a choice, whereas in the election of a chairman of a standing committee, a majority of the whole number of votes given was required.

The meetings of the assembly were held in the school-house, generally known at this time as the " Public Institute," which appears to have been devoted to various public uses. On the 17th of March, the assembly resolved by vote " that the Public Institute, by order of this House, be appropriated as a court room temporarily, until suitable accommodations can be had, unless the same should be wanted for a public school ;" and on the 19th a committee of the assembly was appointed to inform the Rev. Mr. Hunt that it was at his disposal for religious services on Wednesday and Saturday evenings. Prior to the first of November, 1848, there

had been no regularly established Protestant church at San
Francisco. Only occasional Protestant services had been held
there. At this time, however, "the Rev. T. D. Hunt who
had been invited from Honolulu was chosen Protestant chap-
lain to the citizens."[1] He was given a salary of twenty-five
hundred dollars a year to be paid out of subscriptions by the
people of the town.

On this evening, moreover, March 19, 1849, Mr. Hubbard
introduced a bill into the legislative assembly to abolish the
office of alcalde, which, as amended, came up for a third reading March 22, and was passed unanimously. It enacted that
all powers vested in the office of alcalde should cease to be in
force in the town and district of San Francisco, and the office
be abolished; and "that Myron Norton, Esq., having received
the highest number of votes at the election of justices, held on
the twenty-first of February of the present year, shall be and
he is hereby appointed, authorized and empowered to act* as,
exercise and execute the power, duty and office of, police magistrate of the town and district of San Francisco, for the time
being, and to receive from the alcalde all books, records, papers
and documents whatsoever relating to his office and belonging
to the said town and district, in his possession, who shall safely
keep the same until otherwise directed by this legislative
assembly." The police magistrate was required by the terms
of the act to begin the exercise of his duties on the 25th of
March, 1849, and he was empowered to appoint two or more
policemen, who might arrest any person upon a warrant issued
by the magistrate. The police department thus created sup-
planted the constables, sheriffs, and other officers established
under the alcalde who, by this act, were declared dismissed.
Any person "assuming to serve any writ or process" within
the district, except by order and under the authority of the
police magistrate and justices, became liable to a fine of one
hundred dollars; and any one except the police magistrate and

---

[1] Annals, 207.

the justice of the district assuming to issue any writ or process within the district, after the 25th of March, would become liable to a fine of not less than one hundred nor more than five hundred dollars—one-half of the fine going to the informer, and the remainder to the use of the district. To make the transfer of power from the alcalde's government to that of the legislative assembly complete, it was voted, March 26, that the committee of expenditures should "be constituted a select committee to audit the accounts of T. M. Leavenworth, the *late* alcalde of this district, and the said district and town of San Francisco." At the same meeting a bill was passed establishing the office of district attorney, and C. T. Botts was elected by ballot to fill the office thus created. Mr. Botts, however, declined the office, and at the meeting of the legislative assembly, held March 29, George Hyde was unanimously elected. Mr. Hyde was willing to accept the office, but thought he should first resign his seat in the assembly. This body, however, resolved that there would "be no impropriety in the district attorney continuing to be a member of the legislative assembly."

Although during the three months of its existence, the legislative assembly met no less than thirty-five times, yet on many of these occasions it was not possible to transact business because of the lack of a quorum. This was the case on the evening of March 23, and on the evening of April 2. On April 3, a quorum was finally secured, and a bill was then passed establishing the office of Harbor Master, which was filled on the same evening by the election of Capt. E. A. King. The absence of members finally became so serious an evil that, on the 9th of April, Mr. Swasey offered a resolution to the effect "that in the opinion of this Assembly, the continued absence of some of its members shows a lack of duty towards the people and a disrespect to this body." This resolution, although adopted unanimously at the meeting on the 10th of April, did not remove the evil, and near the end of April it was determined to increase the number of representatives in the legislative assembly to twenty-five, with the expectation "that if ten new members were added, a quorum might be obtained for the transaction of business." The ten additional members, having been duly elected, appeared May 14, and took the oath of office.[1]

Almost from the beginning of its history the legislative assembly had agitated the project of forming a general code of laws for the town and district of San Francisco. Such a code was finally passed on the 10th of April, 1849. Among other effects, it established a Justice's Court for the trial of causes; it regulated the practice in the Courts of law; it constituted a Criminal Court for the district of San Francisco; it also established a Court of Appeals for the same district; it established the office of Register in the district of San Francisco, fixed the rates of salaries, and determined certain regulations touching the descent and distribution of intestate estates.

Besides the Police Court, there existed, therefore, under the authority of the legislative assembly, after the adoption of

---

[1] The manner in which the number of members was increased may be seen from the following resolutions taken from the minutes of the meeting of May 3:

" _Whereas_, The necessary business of this Legislative Assembly has been frequently delayed, to the detriment of the good people of this District, by reason of the absence and non-attendance of its members; and whereas, it is believed that if ten new members be added, a quorum may be obtained for the transaction of business, therefore,

" _Resolved_, That the people of the District of San Francisco be requested, at the next election to be held in this district, to vote for ten new members to said body, who shall be qualified to their office at the next meeting of the Assembly succeeding the close of the election.

" _Resolved_, That the people be requested to signify on their respective votes at the said election, by the words 'Aye' or 'No,' their consent or dissent that the ten new members be added, and if it be found that a majority has expressed in favor thereof, the members elect to be qualified and take their seats, and not otherwise." This last provision appears to have been somewhat modified by a later resolution of the Assembly, "that the words _in favor of an addition of ten to the number of the Assembly_, or _against the addition of ten to the number of the Assembly_, be the form to be printed on the votes at the next election."

the Code, a Court of Appeals, the Orphans' Court, and the Criminal Court. The judges of these three Courts were William M. Stewart, of the first, Theron R. Perley, of the second, and Myron Norton, of the third. But in spite of the great legislative activity of the Assembly, the affairs of the revenue and the expenditure remained throughout the three months of its existence in an unsettled and unsatisfactory condition.[1]

About six weeks after the organization of the legislative assembly, April 13, 1849, General Bennet Riley became military governor of California. On the fourth of the following June, he issued a proclamation to the people of the district of San Francisco, stating that proof had been laid before him that a body of men styling themselves "the Legislative Assembly of the District of San Francisco," had "usurped powers which are vested only in the Congress of the United States by making laws, creating and filling offices, imposing and collecting taxes without the authority of law, and in violation of the Constitution of the United States, and of the late treaty with Mexico;" and warning all persons "not to countenance said illegal and unauthorized body, either by paying taxes or by supporting or abetting their officers." He had, moreover, received due proof "that a person assuming the title of sheriff, under the authority of one claiming to be a justice of the peace in the town of San Francisco, did, on the 31st of May last, with an armed party, violently enter the office of the 1st Alcalde of the District of San Francisco, and there forcibly take and carry away the public records of

---

[1] For a record of the organization and acts of the Legislative Assembly, see "Executive Documents," No. 17, House of Representatives, 1st Session, 31st Congress, p. 728; Dwinelle, "Colonial History of San Francisco," Addenda, No. LXXIII; "Minutes of the Proceedings of the Legislative Assembly of the District of San Francisco, from March 12, 1849, to June 4, 1849, and a Record of the Proceedings of the Ayuntamiento or Town Council of San Francisco, from August 6, 1849, until May 3, 1850," San Francisco, 1860, pp. 5–46.

said district from the legal custody and keeping of said 1st Alcalde." In view of this unlawful act, he called upon all good citizens to assist in restoring the records to their lawful keeper, and in sustaining the legally-constituted authorities of the land.

"The office of justice of the peace in California," the proclamation continues, "even where regularly constituted and legally filled, is subordinate to that of alcalde; and for one holding such office to assume the control of, and authority over, a superior tribunal, argues an utter ignorance of the laws, or a wilful desire to violate them, and to disturb the public tranquillity. It is believed, however, that such persons have been led into the commission of this rash act through the impulse of the moment, rather than any wilful and settled design to transgress the law; and it is hoped that on due reflection they will be convinced of their error, and unite with all good citizens in repairing the violence they have done to the laws. It can hardly be possible that intelligent and thinking men should be so blinded by passion, and so unmindful of their own interests and the security of their property, after the salutary and disinterested advice and warnings which have been given them by the President of the United States, by the Secretaries of State and of War, and by men of high integrity and disinterested motives, as to countenance and support any illegally constituted body in their open violation of the laws, and assumption of authority which in no possible event could ever belong to them.

"The office of alcalde is one established by law, and all officers of the United States have been ordered by the President to recognize and support the legal authority of the person holding such office; and whatever feelings of prejudice or personal dislike may exist against the individual holding such office, the office itself should be sacred. For any incompetency or mal-administration, the law affords abundant means of remedy and punishment—means which the Executive will always be found ready and willing to employ, to the full extent of the powers vested in him."[1]

This proclamation denouncing as an illegal body the legislative assembly which for three months had performed all the functions of a town government, was followed the next day, June 5, by an order from Governor Riley, restoring the ayuntamiento to power. This order was based on the well grounded opinion that all the laws of California existing at the time the country was annexed to the United States, which were not in conflict with the constitution, laws, and treaties of the United States, were still in force and must continue in force till changed by competent authority. The powers and duties of all civil officers remained as they had been before the conquest, except so far as they might have been modified by the act of annexation. This order by which the legislative assembly was set aside and power was restored to the council or ayuntamiento, affirmed the traditional power of the council over the lands of the pueblo.

The last meeting of the legislative assembly was held on the 4th of June, and the election ordered by Governor Riley took place on the 1st of August. At this election there were 1,516 votes cast, of which John W. Geary, candidate for the office of first alcalde, received the whole number. Frank Turk, who was elected second alcalde, received 1,055 votes. The ayuntamiento or town council elected at this time consisted of twelve members, namely: Talbot H. Green, Henry A. Harrison, Alfred J. Ellis, Stephen C. Harris, Thomas B. Winton, John Townsend, Rodman M. Price, William H. Davis, Bezer Simmons, Samuel Brannan, William M. Stewart and Gabriel B. Post. Horace Hawes was elected prefect, and Francis Guerrero and Joseph R. Curtis were elected sub-prefects. Peter H. Burrett was elected judge of the Supreme Court.

---

[1] Executive Document No. 17, House of Rep., First Session, 31st Congress, p. 773.

At the second meeting of the newly elected council, Mr. Geary, the first alcalde, spoke at length on the affairs of the town, and asked the co-operation of the council "in making it, in point of order and security, what it must shortly be in wealth and importance, the first city, and great commercial and moneyed emporium of the Pacific."[1]

"Economy in the expenditure of public money," he said, "is at all times desirable and necessary ; but situated as we are here, without any superior body to legislate for us, the people of the city will, of necessity, be called upon to assume a responsibility in the enactment of laws, and in the expenditure of money for public purposes, not usual under ordinary circumstances." The city was, at this time, without a dollar in the public treasury ; there was neither an office for the magistrate, nor any other public edifice. "You are," continued the alcalde, "without a single police officer or watchman, and have not the means of confining a prisoner for an hour ; neither have you a place to shelter, while living, sick and unfortunate strangers who may be cast upon our shores, or to bury them when dead. Public improvements are unknown in San Francisco. In short, you are without a single requisite necessary for the promotion of prosperity, for the protection of property, or for the maintenance of order."

In view of this condition of things, it was clear that the most important question to be considered by the new government was the question of taxation, and to this the alcalde directed a large part of his address. "There is perhaps no city upon the earth," he said, "where a tax for the support of its municipal government can be more justly imposed than here. Real estate, both improved and unimproved, within a short space of time, has increased in value in many instances a thousand-fold, and even at its present high rates, will produce in the shape of rents the largest average income upon

---

[1] Minutes of the Ayuntamiento, August 8, 1849. The address is printed in the "Annals," but it is there set down as delivered at the first meeting.

record. Yet notwithstanding this unprecedented increased value of real estate, the burdens of government should not be borne by a tax upon that species of property alone; each and every kind of business carried on within the limits of the district should bear its just and proper share of taxation.

"The charters of most cities in the United States, granted by the legislature, give the corporation the right to levy and collect a tax, as well to defray the expenses of its municipal government as for public improvements; and it is usual to submit a tax bill to the legislature for its confirmation. This is done to prevent abuses. Yet I do not know of an instance where the tax imposed has been reduced by the legislature. In towns not incorporated there is no resort to be had to the legislature for a confirmation of the tax laws. The town officers, chosen by the people, impose the taxes, and collect a sufficient revenue by common consent; and their right to do so is never questioned. That you have a right to levy and collect a reasonable and proper tax, for the support of your municipal government, cannot, in my judgment, for a moment be questioned. In the absence of State legislative authority you, as the representatives of the people, are supreme in this district, and your acts, so long as you confine them strictly to the legitimate sphere of your duty, will not only be sanctioned and approved by the present worthy executive of our government in California, but will be most promptly confirmed by the legislature, whenever one shall be assembled either for the Territory or State.

"I would, therefore, recommend that with all convenient despatch, you ascertain, as near as possible, the amount of funds deemed necessary for the support of a proper and efficient municipal government for one year; that when you shall have determined this, you shall proceed to collect a just, equitable tax upon real estate and upon sales at auction; and that you require all merchants, traders, storekeepers, etc., to take out a license for the transaction of their business, paying therefor an amount proportionate to the quantity of merchandise vended

by them. Also, that all drays, lighters, and boats, used in
the transportation of merchandise, and of passengers, to or
from vessels in the harbor, be licensed.

" There is also another class of business proper to be taxed,
which although sometimes prohibited by law, yet in many
countries is regulated by law. I recommend you to adopt the
latter course. The passion for gambling is universal, even
where the severest penalties are imposed to prevent its indul-
gence. And it is a fact well known and understood, whenever
gaming tables are licensed and subject to proper police regulations, they are less injurious to the interests and morals of the
community than when conducted in defiance of law. In the
one case the proprietors are amenable to the law which authorizes them, and are subject to proper control, while on the other
hand, if prohibited, the evasion of the law by such means as
are usually resorted to, does but increase the evil, and the
community is in no way benefited. I would, therefore, recommend, under present circumstances, and until State legislation
can be had on the subject, that you license gaming and billiard
tables."

In this address, the alcalde, moreover, urged the council to
adopt measures for the promotion of popular education, in
order that California, when erected into a State, might show
the older States of the Union " that she fully appreciates education as the only safeguard of our republican institutions."
He also called attention to the fact that " the public documents
containing all the muniments of title, etc., for real estate,"
were not to be found in official but in private hands, and
asked for " authority to appoint a committee of three respect-
able and intelligent citizens, who, under oath, shall make an
inventory of the said documents, and a schedule of any muti-
lation, erasures, or interlineations which may be found on
their pages."

But the council had already anticipated this suggestion of
the alcalde's address, for at the first meeting on the 6th of
August, two days before the address was read, the president

4

of the council had been authorized to appoint three commissioners to take an inventory of all public documents which might be turned over to them by the late alcalde, or any other persons. The resolution conveying this authority provided further that the commissioners should not be members of the council.[1] These commissioners were subsequently appointed, and by a resolution of the council, passed August 20, the pay of one of them, Mr. Toler, was fixed at sixteen dollars a day, and that of the other at ten dollars a day.

At an adjourned meeting, the third held by the newly elected town council, the oath of office was administered to Mr. Horace Hawes as prefect, who took the occasion to address the council on the powers and duties of the government which had just been organized.

"Under the peculiar circumstances of this district," he said, "with a population composed of recent immigrants, who, owing to that fact, must necessarily be unacquainted, to a great extent, with the existing laws, it may not be inappropriate for me to allude briefly to those provisions which define our respective functions; and I would remark in passing, that the laws now in force in this country, when well understood, may not be found so inadequate to the purposes of good government as has generally been supposed. It is, perhaps, the abuses and mal-administration which may have existed under the former government, rather than any defect in the laws themselves, which have brought them into disrepute.

"The duties of prefects, though enumerated in twenty-nine separate articles of the code, which will shortly be placed in your hands, may be briefly expressed. They are 'to take care of public order and tranquillity; to publish and circulate, without delay, observe, enforce, and cause to be observed and enforced, the laws throughout their respective districts; and for the execution of these duties, they are clothed with certain

---

[1] Minutes of the Ayuntamiento from August 6, 1849, to May 3, 1850.

powers which are clearly specified and defined. They are particularly enjoined to attend to the subject of public instruction, and see that common schools be not wanting in any of the towns of their respective districts; they are also required to propose measures for the encouragement of agriculture and all branches of industry, instruction, and public beneficence, and for the execution of new works of public utility and the repair of old ones; they constitute the ordinary channel of communication between the governor and the authorities of the district, and are to communicate all representations coming from the latter, accompanied with the necessary information.'

"The general subjects of your charge, gentlemen, are the police, health, comfort, ornament, order and security of your jurisdiction, and you will perceive from an examination of the laws on the subject, that you are invested with extensive powers as respects the various matters upon which you are to act; and when we consider the probable destiny of the infant city, for which you have accepted the office of guardians, in respect to population, wealth and commercial greatness, the prudent exercise of those powers becomes a subject of incalculable importance. In all arrangements and improvements · that are to be permanent, it will be well to take into view the interests, not only of the present, but of future ages; to regard San Francisco, not merely in its present condition, but in its *progress* and the maturity of its greatness. By a prospective view, behold it not only the commercial metropolis of the west, but for beauty and ornament, and the beneficence of its arrangements and institutions, the *model city.*

"Although the lapse of time and the possession of public resources, not now at your disposal, will be indispensable to fulfil these expectations, and it will be for posterity to enjoy and to realize what you have contemplated, you will have it in your power, at least, to prevent any obstacles being interposed that might retard or effectually hinder your city from attaining a destiny so happy and so glorious. From this single view you will perceive the importance of the functions which you have to fulfil. You act as Town Council only, it is true, but the subject of your charge is to be regarded in its important relations to the State, to the republic, and to the commercial world. Every American citizen will feel that he has an interest in it, and will look to the results of your prudent councils with pride and satisfaction. Your being the first Town Council regularly organized under the American Government, your proceedings will be reviewed by succeeding ones in all future time, and regarded with satisfaction, or with regret, as they may have facilitated or retarded the prosperity of the place."[1]

At the same meeting in which Mr. Hawes addressed the council, a number of standing committees were named by the chair: on judiciary, on finance, on streets and public improvements, on police and health, and on expenditures. On the 13th the council appointed a number of municipal officers. Frank Turk was made secretary; William M. Eddy, city surveyor; P. C. Landers, collector of taxes; Jonathan Code, sergeant-at-arms; Malachi Fallon, captain of police; A. C. Peachy, city attorney. Subsequently, on the 20th, Benjamin Burgoyne was elected city treasurer; Dr. J. R. Palmer, city physician; and at the same time the alcalde announced that, in compliance with the instructions of the council, he had appointed John E. Townes sheriff, who had given the required bond in the sum of twenty-five thousand dollars.

The report made by the committee on finance as to the most expedient means for raising a revenue, was adopted on the 27th of August, and, after various modifications, became the basis of a financial policy for the city. It established "a percentage duty on the sales of merchandise and real estate, and imposed heavy license duties on those engaged in different kinds of business."[2] This ordinance having been brought to

---

[1] "Minutes of the Proceedings of the Legislative Assembly and of the Ayuntamiento or Town Council," pp. 221–223.

[2] Annals, 234.

the notice of the prefect, Mr. Hawes, he returned it to the council with his objections fully stated. In the prefect's view it was in conflict with the laws; it imposed taxes which were unequal and disproportioned to the circumstances and abilities of those having to pay them; it was calculated to weigh most heavily and injuriously upon those of limited capital and resources, who ought to receive encouragement and protection; the amount of revenue it would produce was far beyond the needs of the town. In the ordinance imposing the tax there was no specification of the objects to which the revenue was to be applied, and the tax-payers should know for what purpose their money is required. Two main objections are thus raised against the proposed taxes. In the first place, they were excessive. In the second place, they would fall unequally on the tax-payers, and disproportionately to their ability to pay. "Revenue laws," says the prefect, "should be so adjusted as to foster industry and encourage labor, by freeing it from all unnecessary burdens. But this ordinance does precisely the reverse. It makes the drayman pay a tax of eighty dollars a year—probably as much as his cart and mule will be worth at the end of that period—that is, it taxes him to the full amount of his capital. The boatman is taxed upon precisely the same scale. The ordinance takes the whole capital of both, and gives them only the use of it for one year, worth, according to the customary rate of interest here, twelve per cent. The tax upon auction sales, being proportioned to the amount, is more just and equal, but much too high for the wants of the treasury. That imposed upon merchants and traders, however, is glaringly unequal and disproportioned. The wholesale dealer, with a capital of $150,000, will have to pay $400 a year, or about two and two-thirds mills on a dollar, while the small trader, who occupies a tent or shed, with a capital of no more than one thousand dollars, will pay three hundred dollars a year, or thirty-three and one-third dollars on a hundred—that is, the latter will pay a little over one hundred and twenty times as much in proportion to his ability as the former. The pedlar, who is not able to invest above one hundred dollars at once, perhaps, will pay six hundred dollars, or about twenty-four hundred times as much as the first mentioned. Supposing a monte bank, which pays a tax of six hundred dollars a year, by this ordinance, to have ten thousand dollars employed; then, as between the itinerant trader and the gambler, the patronage of the council is in favor of the gambler by one hundred to one—that is, the former has to pay, relatively, one hundred times as much as the latter." Besides these fundamental objections, the prefect finds still others, the most noteworthy of which is the severity of the punishment inflicted on hawkers and pedlars who ply their trade without a license. The ordinance, he observes, " makes the act of peddling without a license, whether from ignorance of the ordinance or a design to violate it, a misdemeanor, but subjects the offender to a total forfeiture of all his goods and chattels; ' for all the goods, wares, merchandise, provisions, or clothing found in his possession at the time of his arrest,' will, in most cases, include all the property he has in the world."

The message containing these objections was received and read before the council at the meeting on the 10th of September, 1849, and at an adjourned meeting two days later, the ordinance for revenue was taken up and amended. A committee was then appointed to wait on Governor Riley and ask for his approval of the bill. The amended articles from 1 to 8 inclusive were, in the governor's opinion, "in strict accordance with the laws and customs of the country." In the same communication the governor also expressed the opinion that the prefect had no power to veto ordinances passed by the town council, it being the duty of the prefect, to use the governor's words, " to exercise, in the administration and expenditure of municipal funds, such supervision as may be granted to him by the ordinances of the ayuntamiento; and in case they exceed their authority, he must report the fact to the governor."

Much of the confusion which appeared in the local affairs

of San Francisco, and of the uncertainty as to the powers
and functions of the officers was due to the fact that California remained without a strictly and clearly defined legal
status under the dominion of the United States. At the
time of the election of the town council which succeeded the
legislative assembly, there were also elected at San Francisco
five delegates to the convention called to frame a constitution
for California. These were Edward Gilbert, Myron Norton,
Wm. M. Gwin, Joseph Hobson, and Wm. M. Stewart. The
convention met in Monterey on the 1st of September, completed its work on the 13th of October, and the constitution
was adopted by popular vote on the 13th of November. It
was not until late in the following year, however, the 9th of
September, 1850, that California was admitted to the Union
as a State. But at the time of the adoption of the constitution a full list of State officers had been elected, and a political organization was formed long before the Congress had
finished wrangling over the question of admission. It was the
legislative department of this unauthorized organization that,
on April 15, 1850, passed the first city charter of San Francisco.

The last ayuntamiento under the old order of things was
elected on the 8th of January, in which John W. Geary was
re-elected first alcalde, and Frank Turk second alcalde. A
number of the members of the previous council were also
re-elected. The new council met on the 11th of January.
The prefect administered the oath of office to Mr. Geary as
first alcalde, who in turn administered it to the members of
the council. The former secretary, Henry L. Dodge, was
unanimously elected to the same position, and after he had
taken the oath of office, the council was declared organized.
The business devolving on the council was executed through
a number of standing committees: on the judiciary, on health
and police, on finance, on expenditures, and on streets, and
public buildings, and public improvements. There was also
appointed a committee on education, to whom were referred
all matters relating to common schools and public education.

Aside from the details of the current business of a rapidly increasing community, two questions of special importance occupied the attention of the municipal officers, between the time of the organization of the council and the 3d of May, the time of its last meeting. These were the question of the land grants and the question relative to the formation of a charter for the city.

On the 21st of December, 1849, the ayuntamiento having learned "that J. Q. Colton, a justice of the peace for the town of San Francisco, had assumed the authority and pretended to exercise the right of selling, granting and disposing of lots within the limits of the town," resolved, therefore, to institute legal proceedings against him in order "to restrain him in such illegal and unwarrantable practices, and to make him amenable, by due process of law, for a misdemeanor and malfeasance in office." A similar charge was also brought against Mr. Leavenworth, sometime alcalde of San Francisco. In the meeting of the council, held December 24, it was resolved to declare "all grants of town lots made and signed by J. Q. Colton, void and of no effect." On the 19th of February, 1850, Horace Hawes, the prefect of San Francisco, addressed a note to the ayuntamiento enclosing a communication from Peter H. Burnett, who had been elected governor of California at the time of the adoption of the constitution, and who had then assumed the authority hitherto held by Governor Riley. This communication ordered that no further sales of the municipal lands be made until the further order of the executive, or until the Legislature should have passed some Act in reference to them. In this order Burnett defines himself as "Governor of the State of California," and yet California was not within six months of admission to the Union. In opposition to this view of the prefect and the governor stands the conclusion reached by the city attorney, A. C. Peachy, in a report made to the ayuntamiento on the 25th of February. After a somewhat minute examination of Mexican law on the point in question, he reached the conclusion "that all lands in the vicinity of the old mission of San Francisco de Asis, and the landing of Yerba Buena, not included in the legal grants to private individuals, or in reserves made by the government, belong · to the municipality of San Francisco, and are subject to be sold at public aution, or granted in *solares* or building lots, in the manner directed by law."

The town council regarded with great disfavor the interference of the governor in the sale of town lots, and on the 25th of February, 1850, resolved "that in our opinion the governor of California has no right to interfere in the sale of town lots." The sale which had been fixed for the 4th of March was postponed until the 4th of April. The council, however, wished to have it understood that in postponing the sale they were not actuated by any fear of the governor of the State interfering in the sale, but that they did it because they wished that those who were anxious to purchase lots might have time to enquire into the powers of the council in the matter. They wished, moreover, to have it understood that they considered the interference of the governor "to be a high-handed act of usurpation on his part, and one in which neither the law nor the opinion of the public sustains him." The original resolutions from which this quotation is derived were finally set aside by the following substitutes, which were passed:

"*Resolved*, That the Constitution of the State of California prescribes the duties, and limits the powers, of the governor; and therefore this council recognize no power in the executive to interfere in their municipal affairs.

"*Resolved*, That any attempt so to interfere, under the pretense that such right is the prerogative of the governor, *ex officio*, or belongs to him as the executive of Mexican law, is inconsistent with the provisions of the constitution, and is an assumption of power dangerous to the rights and liberties of the people."[1]

---

[1] Proceedings of the Ayuntamiento or town council, March 2, 1850.

Through a communication read before the ayuntamiento at the meeting of February 25, the prefect demanded information on certain points:

"*First,* How many, and what water and town lots have been sold by the ayuntamiento since the 1st of August last, the date of the sale, price paid for each lot, and the name of the purchaser, with the terms of payment.

"*Second,* How many of the said town lots, if any, have been originally purchased by members of the ayuntamiento, at sales, public or private, ordered by that body.

"*Third,* Whether, by the resolutions ordering the public sale made on the 3d of January, or any other public sale of said lots, it was provided that a credit should be given for the purchase-money, and if so, whether notice that such credit would be allowed was given to the public in the printed advertisements of such sale.

"*Fourth,* Whether on the night of the 7th January last, the night preceding the election for members of the ayuntamiento, several of the old members met and resolved to appropriate $200,000 for building a wharf at the foot of California street, and if so, who of such members were present at such meeting, and who presided thereat.

"*Fifth,* Whether the water lots adjoining the line of the proposed wharf were purchased by the same members who made the appropriation, and when."

The prefect had informed the ayuntamiento that on the 1st of March a full and complete account, as required by law must be rendered by them, of their administration of the municipal funds, in order that it might be forwarded to the governor and published for the information of the people. It does not, however, appear that the account was rendered in accordance with this request or that satisfactory reply was made to the prefect's list of questions. The communication containing them was read before the council and laid on the table.

The required account not having been received, and the

advertised sales of municipal lands not having been postponed, the prefect appeared in a somewhat excited state of mind: " Your Excellency," he wrote, " will therefore perceive that an issue is clearly presented between the ayuntamiento of San Francisco and the constituted executive authorities of the State. The question to be decided before this community, and before the people of the State is, whether the arbitrary will of the members of the town council or the laws of the land, supported by the executive authorities, shall be the rule in the administration of public affairs." At the same time he demanded definite instructions for his " governance in this crisis," and stated, moreover, that in his view the general sentiment of the citizens of San Francisco was opposed to a further sale of town lots, and that in the " depressed state of monetary affairs, a forced sale would be attended with immense sacrifice of present and future values to the town."

Two days after this writing, Governor Burnett directed the attorney-general of California to aid the prefect and sub-prefect in an examination of the law, with the view: " first, to file a bill in chancery against the ayuntamiento for such accounts as the law requires them to make out and transmit to the sub-prefect; second, to file a bill in chancery to restrain the town council from completing the sales of lots made after the issuing of my order suspending the sales, and from collecting any of the money due upon obligations given for the purchase of such lots; third, to file a bill in chancery to set aside all the purchases of town lots made by any member of the town council before or since the issuing of my orders." In this communication, the governor left the prefect, after consultation with the attorney-general, to take what steps he might deem requisite, and confessed that he had no power to suspend the ayuntamiento except by the consent of the Legislature.

The conflict of authorities which threatened to be serious was finally averted by the retirement of the ayuntamiento. On the 15th of March, 1850, E. J. C. Kewen, the attorney-general, wrote to Governor Burnett in a somewhat exultant tone of victory : " The enemy have fled, and we are the sole occupants of the field. The sale is indefinitely postponed. I advised Hawes to exert the authority of his office to the utmost extent that law would justify, and in the event of failing to accomplish the desired end, I should have proceeded without further delay upon a writ of *quo warranto*. They are evidently fearful of any action that will cause an investigation into the extent of their authority, and catching some hint of ulterior proceedings in contemplation, in case of disobedience to executive behests, they have exposed the character of the beast that paraded so ostentatiously in the lion's skin."[1]

The prefect, by this victory, did not achieve lasting glory. On the 29th of March, 1850, he was suspended by Governor Burnett on charges preferred by the ayuntamiento of San Francisco. The *Alta California* of April 1, commenting on the governor's action, stated it as a matter of notoriety that Prefect Hawes had " been continually annulling the acts of the ayuntamiento, and sending forth complaints and pronunciamentos against them," and "that he had it in contemplation to assume the entire control of the town affairs."

Further investigation of the supposed frauds in connection with the sale of land within the limits of the town were deferred to a later time.

At a meeting of the ayuntamiento, December 1, 1849, Samuel Brannan moved to authorize the alcalde to appoint a day for the election of eleven delegates to draft a city charter to be presented to the State Legislature for adoption. This motion was lost; but on the 12th of the same month he offered a resolution of a somewhat similar purport, which was adopted. This second resolution, however, provided that the committee of five to draft the charter should be appointed by the chair. Messrs. Brannan, Davis, Turk, Harrison and Price were appointed, and by a subsequent resolution they

---

[1] " Minutes of the Ayuntamiento, 1849–1850," p. 237.

were authorized to examine and define the extent of territory to be embraced within the limits of the city. This committee failed to perform the work required of it, and at a meeting of the ayuntamiento, January 16, 1850, the committee on judiciary was instructed to submit a charter to the council on the 28th of the month, which, if approved, would be presented to the citizens on the first Monday of February. This committee was authorized to procure such legal advice and assistance as they might deem advisable, to aid them in drafting the charter in accordance with their instructions. The charter as formed by the judiciary committee was submitted to the council on the 30th of January, 1850. It was read by sections, amended and adopted. It was then referred back to the committee to be engrossed, and the committee was instructed to have five hundred copies of it printed and distributed among the citizens of San Francisco. On the 13th of February a special meeting of the ayuntamiento or council was called for the reconsideration of the charter. As amended at this meeting, in a committee of the whole, it was finally adopted by a vote of four to three. Messrs. Hagan and Green were then requested to present it to the San Francisco representatives in the Legislature that it might be adopted by that body.

A few weeks later, March 11, the Legislature passed a general Act providing for the incorporation of cities. Under this Act any city in the State, of at least two thousand inhabitants, might be incorporated, either by the Legislature or by the County Court, upon application. The outline of a charter embraced in this Act provided for a government by a mayor, recorder and common council, who should possess the power usually belonging to a municipal government. Before the passage of this general law, an Act had been passed, February 27, to incorporate Sacramento City. Benicia, San Diego and San José were incorporated on March 27. Three days later, March 30, an Act was passed incorporating Monterey, and on the 4th of April Sonoma and Los Angeles were added to the list. The incorporation of Santa Barbara followed, April 9, and that of San Francisco on April 15. San Francisco was thus the ninth city of California incorporated after the adoption of the Constitution.

III.

The territory embraced within the boundaries fixed by the charter of 1850, was only a small part of that to which the city was entitled, according to later judicial decisions. The southern boundary of this territory was a line parallel to Clay street and two miles distant, in a southerly direction, from the centre of Portsmouth Square. The western boundary was a line one mile and a half distant, in a westerly direction, from the centre of Portsmouth Square, running parallel to Kearney street. The northern and eastern boundaries were the same as those of the county of San Francisco. This was a limitation for the purposes of municipal administration, but it was provided that it should not be " construed to divest or in any manner prejudice any right or privilege to which the city of San Francisco may be entitled beyond the limits above described." Provision was made for dividing the city into eight wards, which could not be altered, increased, or diminished in number except by the action of the Legislature. The division was to be made by the first council elected under the charter, and was to be so made that there should be in each ward, as near as might be, the same number of white male inhabitants. The government of the city was vested in a mayor, recorder, and common council, the council consisting of a board of aldermen and a board of assistant aldermen. Each board was composed of one member from each ward, had the right to elect its president, and was in the enjoyment of all those privileges and prerogatives which usually pertain to a legislative assembly. Under the charter, moreover, provision was made for a treasurer, comptroller, street commissioner, collector of city taxes, city marshal, city attorney, and from each ward two assessors. These offices were all elective, and the time fixed for the election was the fourth Monday of April in each year. The elections were ordered by the common council, whose duty it was to designate the place of holding them ; to give at least ten days' notice of the same ; and to appoint inspectors of election at each place of voting. Returns of all elections were made to the common council, who issued certificates of election to the persons chosen. A plurality of votes was required for election. The elections were not to be held in a " grog-shop or other place where intoxicating liquors were vended," and the polls were to be open one day " from sunrise till sunset."

The duties of the mayor were " to communicate to the common council at least once in each year" a general statement of the condition of the city with reference to its governmental affairs ; to recommend to the common council the adoption of such measures as he should deem expedient; "to be vigilant and active in causing the laws and ordinances of the city government to be duly executed and enforced ; to exercise a constant supervision and control over the conduct and acts of all subordinate officers ; to receive and examine into all such complaints as may be preferred against any of them for violation or neglect of duty, and certify the same to the common council " for their action. The common council had power to declare the office of any person so complained against vacant if the complaint were found to be true.

The recorder was a judicial officer having, within the limits of the city, essentially the same power as a justice of the peace. He had, moreover, jurisdiction over all violations of the city ordinances. The city marshal was a regular attendant upon the Recorder's Court, and under obligation " to execute and return all processes issued by the recorder, or divested to him by any legal authority." The marshal might appoint one or more deputies who should have equal power with himself; he should arrest all persons guilty of a breach of the peace and of violation of the city ordinances, and bring them before the recorder for trial. He should possess, finally, superintending control of the city police.

The treasurer was required to make out and present to the mayor quarterly "a full and complete statement of the receipts and expenditures of the preceding three months," to be published in a manner to be prescribed by ordinance. The usual oath and bond were required of all city officers before entering upon the duties of their offices, and the mayor, recorder, aldermen and assistant aldermen were required to qualify within three days of their election. The duties of the comptroller, street commissioner, collectors and all other officers whose functions were not laid down in the charter, were to be defined by the common council.

The legislative power was vested in the mayor and the two bodies of the common council. Conspicuous limitations on this power were: 1. That the taxes levied and collected should not exceed one per cent. per annum, upon all property made taxable by law for State purposes; 2. That money borrowed on the faith of the city should "never exceed three times its annual estimated revenues." With respect to all ordinances passed by the common council, the mayor possessed a limited veto which was defined in terms similar to those employed in describing the veto power of the President of the United States. In case of a vacancy in the office of mayor, or in case of the absence or the inability of the mayor, the president of the board of aldermen should exercise the mayor's duties and receive his salary. The mayor might call special sessions of the common council at any time by proclamation, and should state to the members when assembled the purpose for which they had been convened.

In the case of bills appropriating money, imposing taxes, increasing, lessening, or abolishing licenses, or for borrowing money, it was required that the "yeas" and "nays" should be entered on the journals. For the passage of any appropriation bill involving the sum of five hundred dollars or more, and of any bill increasing or diminishing the city revenue, the vote of a majority of all the members elected was required. All resolutions and ordinances, moreover, calling for the appropriation of any sum of money exceeding fifteen thousand dollars, were required to lie over for ten days and be published for one week in at least one public daily paper. It was unlawful for any member of the common council to be interested in any contract, the expenses of which were to be paid out of the city treasury; and the city itself was not permitted to become the subscriber for stock in any corporation.

In case it should become necessary for the city to use private property for laying out, changing, or improving streets, and no agreement between the owners and the corporation should be possible, the property might be taken on the· payment by the city of a. sum fixed by a board of five commissioners appointed by the County Court. In any proposition to pave, grade, light, water, or otherwise improve a street, one-third of the owners of the land opposite the proposed improvements making objection, the improvements should not be made. But if the number of the objectors was less than one-third of the owners, the improvements should be made. The initiative in improvements might also be taken by the owners of property opposite which they were desired. They should be made if three-fourths of the owners required them and applied therefor to the common council, provided there were funds in the treasury not otherwise appropriated that might be used for this purpose.

That there might be no conflict of powers, it was provided by a final section of the charter, that all the powers and functions of all officers whatsoever who had hitherto exercised authority in the municipal government of San Francisco should cease and be determined from and after the day on which the officers prescribed by the charter should be duly elected and qualified.

The first election under this charter was held May 1, 1850, at the time the vote was taken for its adoption by the citizens of San Francisco. The following officers were elected:

Mayor.—John W. Geary.

Recorder.—Frank Tilford.

Marshal.—Malachi Fallon.

City Attorney.—Thos. H. Holt.

Treasurer.—Charles G. Scott.

Comptroller.—Benj. L. Berry.

Tax Collector.—Wm. M. Irvin.

Street Commissioner.—Dennis McCarthy.

Aldermen.

Charles Minturn,	A. A. Selover,	C. W. Stuart,
F. W. Macondray,	Wm. Greene,	Wm. M. Burgoyne,
D. Gillespie,		M. L. Mott.

Assistant Aldermen.

A. Bartol,	John Maynard,	L. T. Wilson,
C. T. Botts,	John P. Van Ness,	A. Morris,
Wm. Sharton,		Wm. Corbett.

Assessors.

Robert B. Hampton,	John H. Gibson,	John P. Haff,
Holsey Brower,	Francis C. Bennett,	Beverly Miller,
John Garvey,		Lewis B. Coffin.

Before the end of the following January several changes occurred in the common council. Mr. Burgoyne was never qualified and Mr. Macondray resigned. Their places were filled on the 27th of June by the election of Moses G. Leonard and John Middleton. Of the assistant aldermen, Mr. Maynard and Mr. Botts resigned, and their places were filled by George W. Green and James Grant. Later changes were effected in the board of aldermen by the retirement of Mr. Gillespie and Mr. Leonard, whose places were filled on the 20th of January, 1851, by the election of W. H. V. Cronise and D. G. Robinson. At the time of this last election, George W. Gibbs was chosen to fill a vacancy in the board of assistant aldermen caused by the resignation of Mr. Morris.

The two boards met to organize and appoint committees on the 9th of May, in the City Hall, at the corner of Kearney and Pacific streets. At these meetings a message from the mayor was received and read. The reports of the treasurer and comptroller submitted at this time show the liabilities of the city to have been $199,174.19, while the assets were $238,253.00, being an excess of $39,078.81 over the liabilities.

The new government having been put into operation shortly after the conflagration of May 4, its attention was directed to the necessity of providing more efficient means for extinguishing fires. To this end an ordinance was passed declaring "that if any person, during a conflagration, should refuse to assist in extinguishing the flames, or in removing goods endangered by fire to a place of safety, he should be fined in a sum not less than five, and not exceeding one hundred dollars." The mayor was authorized "to enter into contracts for digging artesian wells and for the immediate construction of water reservoirs in various parts of the city." Another ordinance passed at an early meeting of the council ordained that every householder should " furnish six water buckets, to be kept always in readiness for use during the occurrence of future fires."

At its first meeting held May 9, 1850, the common council entered upon a scheme for plundering the city treasury in behalf of the members of the government. A bill to fix the salaries of the several city officers was brought forward, discussed, and laid over for subsequent consideration. It was proposed that the mayor, the recorder, the marshal, and the city attorney should receive ten thousand dollars each per annum. The comptroller, the aldermen, and the assistant aldermen were to have six thousand dollars each, while the treasurer was to receive one per cent. of all receipts, and the tax collector three per cent. of all sums collected. This proposition, coupled with an extravagant and unwise license law, awakened a spirit of indignation in the citizens, and "came very near overthrowing the entire city government."[1] Numerous public meetings were held to devise means for putting an end to the disgraceful conduct of the legally constituted authorities. Such a meeting was held in Portsmouth Square, on the evening of June 5, and was attended by several thousand persons. At a previous meeting a committee had been appointed to take into consideration "the acts of the common council upon the subject of taxation and salaries." The committee having canvassed the subject, submitted to the

---

[1] *Daily Alta California*, August 14, 1850.

meeting of June 5, the following resolutions which were adopted:

" *Whereas*, It is customary and proper for the people at all times to assemble and deliberate together upon the acts of their public servants,—and to instruct them when they shall have exceeded their just powers, or imposed unnecessary burdens on the community,—and whereas, the system of oppressive taxation, of high salaries and other impolitic measures, proposed by our present city council, have a sure and certain tendency to retard the growth, to obstruct the commerce, to cripple the industry, and to overload the people of our city,—we, the citizens of San Francisco, in public meeting assembled, do hereby resolve and declare—

" *Resolved*, That while we duly respect the lawfully constituted authorities of our city, and are willing to pay all proper taxes, to meet the necessary public expenses and improvements, we most earnestly protest against the great and unequal pressure of the present scheme of taxation,—against the high salaries proposed, especially for offices considered in other cities offices of trust and honor, and not of profit,—and against the expenditure of the public funds for purposes never contemplated by the votes of this city.

" *Resolved*, That in view of the grievance of which we complain, should the scheme of high salaries be carried out by the common council, we shall view their position as antagonistical ; and we believe that such an act will call forth a popular dissatisfaction, which will render all taxation difficult, depriving our city of necessary revenue, and still further embarrass our already bankrupt treasury.

" *Resolved*, That in the opinion of this meeting, the salaries of all the officers of the city should be limited to the least remunerating rates, and that the common council should receive no salary, except, perhaps, a reasonable *per diem* allowance for extra labors in committees, so long as the corporation is unable to supply its pressing wants and pay its honest debts.

" *Resolved*, That we consider the scale of taxation as proposed and in part established by our city council, not only unjust to all classes, but especially oppressive to the interests of the laboring and poorer classes, and that as hundreds of good citizens are daily arriving in embarrassed circumstances, a heavy tax upon their limited means of honest livelihood is unjust and wrong.

"*Resolved,* That we instruct our mayor and common council to abandon the scheme of high salaries, and to remodel the schedule of oppressive taxation as shadowed forth by their recent actions; and unless they are willing to do so, to resign and give place to more patriotic and efficient men.

"*Resolved,* That a committee of twenty-five be appointed by this meeting to wait upon the common council, with a copy of these resolutions, and request an answer thereto."

These resolutions were presented to the common council at a meeting of that body, held June 7, by J. L. Fulsom, chairman of the committee of twenty-five. They were read, and, by a vote of the council, laid on the table. Alderman Selover, the mover of this action, contended "that they were insulting and not couched in terms which should entitle them to respect and consideration." The vote that the resolutions lie indefinitely on the table was not considered such an answer as was due to the great popular assembly represented by the committee of twenty-five. When, therefore, this committee reported to a subsequent meeting in the public square, on the evening of June 12, they were empowered to increase their number to five hundred, and authorized to present the same resolutions to the council in such form as they might think proper. They were instructed, moreover, to report to a meeting of the people to be held on the 17th of June, and at that time to recommend such course of action as they might deem necessary. "The committee thus fortified, afterwards chose the additional members, and fixed the evening of the 14th, when they should all march in procession to the place of meeting of the common council, and there again submit the 'sovereign will' of the people to the aldermen, and require their prompt obedience to the same. On that day the great conflagration took place; and further action on the subject of the high salaries and obnoxious taxation ordinances was indefinitely postponed. Popular excitement took a new direction in consequence of the fire; and, excepting in the columns of the *Herald* newspaper, and among a few testy individuals, little more was said on the matter till some months afterwards, when the question was revived. The previous meetings, however, had the effect of causing the obnoxious license ordinance to be withdrawn for a time. In the end, the salaries of both the municipal officers and the common council were reduced, the latter being ultimately fixed at four thousand dollars."[1] The salaries of the other municipal officers ranged from eight thousand to ten thousand dollars.

A charter having been adopted, the city proceeded to take

---

[1] The action of the mayor, John W. Geary, in vetoing the ordinance which fixed the salaries of the members of the council at four thousand dollars, "was universally and heartily applauded by the people." In returning the ordinance to the council, unapproved, he called the attention of members to the inexpediency of their action. "With great unanimity," he said, among other things, "a financial measure has been adopted to provide for the immediate payment of the city's indebtedness by means of a loan of half a million of dollars. It is of the greatest importance to the interests of the city that that measure should be made to succeed at the earliest possible moment. In my deliberate judgment its success would be injuriously impeded, if not entirely defeated, by associating with the proposition for a loan, an ordinance to appropriate so large a proportion of the amount demanded as sixty-four thousand dollars, to the payment of a class of officers whose services are usually rendered without any other remuneration than the honor conferred by their fellow-citizens, and their participation in the general good which it is their province and duty to promote. It could not fail to weaken our public credit to show a purpose to use it for the payment of salaries never contemplated by the people, especially in view of the admitted necessity for the practice of the most rigid economy, in order to complete by means of all the resources and credit we possess the public works in progress or in contemplation. With scarcely a dollar in the public treasury—without the means of discharging even the interest falling due for the script already issued—the city credit impaired, and general bankruptcy staring us in the face, retrenchment should be the order of the day, rather than the opening up of new modes of making enormous and heretofore unknown expenditures." "Annals," 280–281. The efforts of the citizens to compel economy in the government did not cease with their opposition to the proposed salaries. On the 24th of June D. R. Smith and others petitioned the council "to investigate the conduct of the street commissioner in hiring a mule at twenty-five dollars per day."

an inventory of its goods. A commission was, therefore, appointed by the common council, consisting of one alderman, one assistant alderman, and one citizen of San Francisco, to ascertain and report to the common council, the extent, description, and condition of all the property belonging to this city, or to the municipality, or pueblo of Yerba Buena, or San Francisco, on the 29th day of April last; and all claims, rights, titles, and interests of said city or pueblo to or in any lands, funds, or property within the corporate limits; and also to ascertain and report upon any right or privilege to which the citizens of San Francisco, or the citizens or inhabitants thereof in common, may be entitled beyond the limits described by the act to incorporate the city of San Francisco.[1]

During its brief and inglorious career, the common council was so completely absorbed in the question of the members' salaries, that the work of organizing the government made only slow progress. It was provided, however, by a joint resolution of the two bodies of the council, that at the beginning of every municipal year certain joint standing committees should be appointed by the council, each board appointing three members of each committee. The committees specified were: 1. on finance; 2. on fire and water; 3. on police, prisons, and health; 4. on streets, wharves, and public buildings; 5. on ordinances; 6. on education; 7. on engrossing; 8. on the judiciary. Each committee was empowered to choose its own chairman by ballot. By another joint resolution of the same date, June 19, 1850, the following method of legislative procedure was established for the council:

"Every ordinance shall have as many readings in each board as the rules of each board may require; after which the question shall be on passing the same to be engrossed, and when the same shall have been passed to be engrossed, it shall be sent to the other board for concurrence; and when such ordinance shall have so passed to be engrossed in each

---

[1] Ordinance dated May 30, 1850.

board, the same shall be engrossed by the clerk of that body in which it originated, and examined by the joint engrossing committee, and upon their report the question shall be in each board, upon its final passage ; upon its final passage in the concurring board it shall be signed by the president thereof and returned to the board in which it originated. Upon its final passage in the originating board, it shall be signed by the president thereof and transmitted to the mayor, by whom it shall be returned with his signature or objections to the board from whence it came."

During the last half of the year several departments were organized, particularly those for whose efforts there was the most imperative need. The fire department was established by an ordinance passed on the first of July. Companies of at least twenty members having adopted and signed a constitution, might petition the common council for apparatus, house and other articles required. The rules of the department were made by an association composed of two delegates from each company, elected on the first Monday of August each year. The rules thus made were regarded as binding by all companies in the department. It was provided there should be a chief engineer and two assistant engineers. They were elected by the members of the several companies. The chief engineer was president of the board of delegates. It was the duty of the chief engineer, moreover, " to superintend the organization of all fire companies in San Francisco; to examine all engines, hose and apparatus belonging thereto, which the city may wish to purchase; to superintend the erection of engine houses and cisterns ; to exercise a general supervision and control over all branches of the fire department of this city ; to act in conjunction with the fire committee, on all subjects which may be referred to them ; and to protect the engines and apparatus of the city which shall be placed in the houses of private companies."

The chief engineer was required also " to superintend and direct the operations of all companies at fires or conflagrations; he was given authority, with the consent of the mayor and two members of the common council, to blow up any building or buildings with gunpowder," which he might deem necessary for the suppression of the fire, or to perform such other acts as might be demanded by the emergency. He was required to report the condition of his department at least once in three months, or oftener if demanded. A bond in the sum of ten thousand dollars was required of him, and his salary was to be six thousand dollars per year, payable monthly.

The police department, as organized under the charter of 1850, consisted of a night and a day police "not to exceed seventy-five men, including captains, assistant captains, sergeants of police, and policemen." They were nominated by the city marshal and confirmed by the mayor. Of this department, the marshal was the chief executive officer, and he was held responsible to the common council "for the efficiency, general conduct and good order of the officers and men."

The city was divided into three police districts, in each of which provision was made for one deputy marshal, or police captain, and one assistant captain, and two police sergeants. Each district was divided into as many beats or stations as were deemed necessary and might be approved by the city marshal. The salaries fixed were ten dollars a day for each captain of police; eight dollars a day for each assistant captain, each sergeant, and each policeman. The salaries were paid semi-monthly by the comptroller through warrants.

The ordinance organizing the street department was approved September 20, 1850, and the department when organized was charged with "opening, regulating, and improving streets, constructing and repairing wharves and piers, digging and building wells and sewers, and the making of public roads, when done by assessment, and all other matters relating to public lands and places, and the assessing and collecting of the amounts required for such expenditures." The work of the department was distributed among three bureaux: 1. The bureau of assessment and collection; 2. The bureau of surveying and engineering; 3. The bureau of wharves and piers. The chief officer of the department was the street commissioner, who by virtue of his office was one of the surveyors of the city. He was required to execute a bond to the corporation in the sum of ten thousand dollars for the faithful performance of his official duties. He made all contracts for work, and all pecuniary obligations of the city under these contracts were met by warrants of the comptroller, drawn upon the requisition of the commissioner. He was required to indicate to the common council, from time to time, the improvements needed, and present plans for making them; in a word, he was to be the manager of the department. The second general officer was called the clerk to the street commissioner, by whom he was appointed and whom he assisted in all matters pertaining to the street department. He kept accounts in relation to all contracts made, prepared the requisitions upon the comptroller for the amounts due the several contractors, examined all claims against the corporation, and kept a record of assessments. In case of vacancy in the office of street commissioner, the clerk was empowered to act in that capacity until the appointment of a new commissioner.

The officers of the bureau of assessment and collection received their appointment "by nomination of the street commissioner, and election by the common council." They were "charged with the duties of making the estimates and assessments required for all public alterations and improvements ordered by the common council," and of collecting all assessments that had been confirmed by the same body. The collector of assessments, in order to insure the faithful performance of his official duties, was required to "execute a bond to the corporation, with at least two sureties, to be approved by the comptroller, in the final sum of twenty-five thousand dollars."

It was provided that the city and county surveyor should

be the chief officer of the bureau of surveying and engineering. The main functions of this bureau were to assist the street commissioner " in laying out and regulating the streets, roads, wharves and slips of the city." It was, moreover, required to lay out and survey ground for the purpose of building, and to advise and direct all relative matters. No person, in fact, was permitted to build on his own land unless the land had previously been " viewed and laid out by the city or county surveyor, with the advice and consent of the street commissioner," and for these services the city surveyor might demand and receive the fees allowed by the legislature to county surveyors, but whenever he was employed by the street commissioner to make a survey, he was to receive compensation at the rate of sixteen dollars a day. For making a survey for the purpose of regulating and improving a street, he was to " receive at the rate of twenty-five dollars for each hundred feet running measure to be thus improved." For other special surveys, as for building a sewer, specific charges were fixed by the ordinance through which the department was organized.

At the head of the bureau of wharves and piers was the superintendent of wharves, whose duty it was to inspect the condition of the public wharves and piers, to repair those existing, and to superintend the erection of new ones. He was nominated by the street commissioner and appointed by the common council, and his bond to the corporation was in the sum of five thousand dollars. Besides superintending the wharves and piers, he was required to advise with the street commissioner in relation to such improvements as might appear necessary, which, being approved, should be reported to the common council with the commissioner's recommendation. In case, however, the proposed improvements should not involve an expense exceeding four hundred dollars, they might be undertaken by the authority of the street commissioner, by whom alone, as in other cases, all requisitions upon the comptroller for payments should be made.

The office of wharfinger was created December 20, 1850. The incumbent was " to have a general superintendence and control of the wharves belonging to the city." He was subordinated to the street commissioner by whom he was nominated. It was his duty to collect all tolls and money accruing from the use of the wharves; and his compensation was to be twenty per cent. of the gross receipts. He was required to give a bond in the amount of three thousand dollars.

According to the provisions of the charter the city was to be divided by the common council into eight wards. This was done by an ordinance dated November 5, 1850. The first ward embraced that portion of the city east of Stockton and north of Jackson street; the second, that portion west of Stockton and north of Jackson; the third, that portion east of Kearney, between Jackson and Sacramento; the fourth, that portion west of Kearney, between Sacramento and Jackson; the fifth, that portion bounded by Sacramento, Market and Kearney streets; the sixth, all that portion west of Kearney, between Sacramento and Market; the seventh, all that portion south and east of Market, and east of Fourth street; and the eighth, all that portion west of Fourth street and south and east of Market.

The municipal government thus created and organized under the charter of 1850, and the whole political organization to which it belonged, occupied a peculiar and anomalous position. California at that time was simply a conquered region which had not been organized by Congress into either a territory or a State. In this position the people, impelled by the necessities of their circumstances, had adopted a constitution and set up a government which had much likeness to the government of a State in the Union. This goverment, however, had not been adopted or recognized by the power which alone held the sovereign authority over this region, and whose coöperation with the inhabitants was necessary to the organization of legitimate political institutions. The city charter was, therefore, an act of an unauthorized body, and it was within the power of the government at Washington to set aside both the charter and the legislative body from which it had proceeded.

The uncertainties of their position led the people of San Francisco to look with eagerness for favorable news from Congress during the months in which the proposition to make California a State was before that body. When the expected tidings finally arrived, on the 18th of October, the inhabitants, to use the language of a contemporary writer, were "half wild with excitement." "Business of almost every description was instantly suspended, the Courts adjourned in the midst of their work, and men rushed from every house into the streets and towards the wharves, to hail the harbinger of the welcome news. When the steamer rounded Clark's Point and came in front of the city, her masts literally covered with flags and signals, a universal shout arose from ten thousand voices on the wharves, in the streets, upon the hills, house-tops, and the world of shipping in the bay. Again and again were huzzas repeated, adding more and more every moment to the intense excitement and unprecedented enthusiasm. Every public place was soon crowded with eager seekers after the particulars of the news, and the first papers issued an hour after the appearance of the Oregon were sold by the newsboys at from one to five dollars each. The enthusiasm increased as the day advanced. Flags of every nation were run up on a thousand masts and peaks and staffs, and a couple of large guns placed upon the plaza were constantly discharged. At night every public thoroughfare was crowded with the rejoicing populace. Almost every large building, all the public saloons and places of amusement were brilliantly illuminated—music from a hundred bands assisted the excitement—numerous balls and parties were hastily got up—bonfires blazed upon the hills, and rockets were incessantly thrown into the air, until the dawn of the following day."[1]

---

[1] "Annals," 293.

In what manner the common council had contributed to the cause of this public rejoicing does not appear; measures were taken, however, through which each member was to receive, nominally as a present from the city, a gold medal, of the value of one hundred and fifty dollars, commemorative of the admission of California to the Union. This scheme, the responsibility for which it was difficult to fix, following as it did on the heels of other manifestations of inordinate greed displayed by the city government, aroused public inquiries as to what services had been rendered by the council that were not adequately covered by their enormous salaries. The outcry that was raised against the project prevented its execution, and the councilmen who received the medals became willing to pay for them, in order that they might hide them as quickly as possible in the melting pot. But even this action did not free them from the imputation of having planned to award themselves costly decorations to be provided from the funds of the city treasury.

That the municipal government was in disreputable hands become apparent very early, and every succeeding month brought forth new evidence of the lamentable fact. During the year 1850, San Francisco had unquestionably improved in appearance. It had grown from a " mass of low wooden huts and tents " to be a city "in great part built of brick houses, with pretty stores; and the streets—formerly covered with mud and water—floored throughout with thick and dry planks." [1] But honesty and efficiency were wanting in the administration of its affairs. The courts were corrupt, and already there were manifestations of that sentiment which found expression in the vigilance committee of the following year. The government appeared to have brought the municipality a long way on the road to financial ruin. On the 25th of March, the editor of the *Daily Alta California* wrote:
" If any other city has had the singular fortune to run in

---

[1] Gerstaecker, " Journey," 243.

debt so deeply in so short a period as San Francisco, we have never heard of it. If any other city has incurred debt so wantonly, without ever considering the means of payment, or making any provision for sustaining its credit, it has not been in our day. Here is a city not three years old, with a population of perhaps 25,000 people owing already one million of dollars, and looking forward with the intensest satisfaction to an accumulating interest of 36 per cent. per annum."

A remedy for the serious ills that had fallen upon the city appeared to lie in the adoption of a new charter, and in the election of a new list of municipal officers. A new charter was clearly needed, not merely because the existing one was a carelessly constructed instrument, but also because it lacked the requisite authority. In order, therefore, to supply the evident deficiencies, the first legislature convened after the admission of California to the Union re-incorporated the city of San Francisco by an act passed on the 15th of April, 1851.

The charter of 1851 retained all the essential forms of the pre-existing government; it differed from that of the previous year in its more careful definition of the functions of the several departments, particularly in its specifications as to financial management. The southern and western boundaries of the city alone were changed. The former was kept parallel to Clay street, but was placed two miles and a half instead of, as formerly, two miles from the centre of Portsmouth square. The western line was placed at a distance of two miles, instead of a mile and a half from the same point, and remained, as formerly, parallel to Kearney street. The existing division of the city into eight wards was adopted, but it was provided that the common council should, " at least three months before the general election of 1852, and also during the second year thereafter redistrict the city, so that each ward " should contain approximately the same number of inhabitants. Instead of the two assessors from each ward provided for by the previous charter, it was here determined that there should be elected annually three for the whole city by a general ticket.

In the charter of 1850, it was provided that of the whole number of sixteen assessors only eight should be elected for the first year, while in that of 1851, it was specified that for the first year only two should be elected.

On the transaction of business by the council, the second charter imposed restrictions unknown to the first. Under the first charter a majority of the members elected constituted a quorum, and an ordinance might be passed by a majority of the members present, which might mean by a majority of a simple quorum. The ayes and nays were taken and entered on the journal only as they might be called for by one or more members; whereas under the second charter no ordinance or resolution could "be passed unless by a majority of all the members elected to each board. On the final passage of every ordinance or resolution ayes and nays shall be taken and entered upon the journal." But in its financial dealings, the council was most completely hedged about, as may be seen from several sections of the third article:

"Every ordinance providing for any specific improvement, the creation of any office, or the granting of any privilege, or involving the sale, lease, or other appropriation of public property, or the expenditure of public moneys (except for sums less than five hundred dollars), or laying any tax or assessment, and every ordinance imposing a new duty or penalty shall, after its passage by either board, and before being sent to the other, be published with the ayes and nays in some city newspaper, and no ordinance or resolution, which shall have passed one board shall be acted upon by the other on the same day, unless by unanimous consent" (Art. III, sec. 4).

With reference to municipal debts, the first charter authorized the common council "to borrow money and pledge the faith of the city therefor, provided the aggregate amount of the debts of the city shall never exceed three times its annual estimated revenues." Notwithstanding the unequivocal limitations of this provision, it was not observed. The debts created by the council of 1850 were more than three times the amount of the annual revenues. In the second charter the line of restriction was more closely drawn. The council could not "create, nor permit to accrue, any debts or liabilities which, in the aggregate with all former debts or liabilities, shall exceed the sum of fifty thousand dollars over and above the annual revenue of the city, unless the same shall be authorized by ordinance for some specific object, which ordinance shall provide ways and means, exclusive of loans, for the payment of the interest thereon as it falls due, and also to pay and discharge the principal within twelve years." To make the security still greater, the principle of *referendum* was here applied, it being determined that this ordinance should not take effect until it had been submitted to the people and received a majority of all the votes cast; and the money thus raised could be used only for the object mentioned in the ordinance, or for the payment of the debt thereby created. It was, however, provided that the existing city debt, with the interest accruing thereon, should make no part of the fifty thousand dollars specified. The council, furthermore, had no power to borrow money unless it should "by ordinance direct the same in anticipation of the revenue for the current year, and should provide in the ordinance for repaying the same out of such revenue;" nor in such case could the sum borrowed exceed fifty thousand dollars. A larger sum might, however, be raised by loan for the purpose of extinguishing the existing liabilities of the city, whenever the ordinance providing for the same should have first been approved by the electors of the city at a general election. On such a loan the yearly rate of interest should not exceed ten per cent., and the whole should be payable within twenty years.

The financial activity of the council was further circumscribed by the prohibition "to emit bills of credit or to issue or put in circulation any paper or device as a representative of value or evidence of indebtedness, to award damage for the non-performance or failure on their part of any contract, to loan the credit of the city, to subscribe to the stock of any association or corporation, or to increase the funded debt of the city unless the ordinance for that purpose were first approved by the people at a general election." With respect to taxation, both charters contained the same provision, limiting the amount that might be imposed by the council to one per cent. a year of the assessed value of the property. This was not an absolute limitation, for the council had power to raise, by tax, any amount of money that it might deem expedient, whenever the ordinance for that purpose had been approved by the people. That there would be occasion for exercising this extraordinary power appeared probable in view of the enormous debt that had been thrust upon the city, and of the rapidly increasing need of public improvements. Yet in spite of the pressing demand for money for current uses, the second charter definitely set aside certain revenues to constitute a sinking fund for the payment of the city debt. As long as the debt remained uncancelled, the funds accruing from these revenues could be used for no other purpose. These revenues were: 1. The net proceeds of all sales of real estate belonging, or that may hereafter belong, to the city; 2. The net proceeds of all bonds and mortgages payable to the city; 3. Receipts "for occupation of private wharves, basins, and piers;" 4. Receipts for wharfage, rents, and tolls. To prevent the common council from voting such extravagant salaries as had been paid to the city officers under the first charter, it was provided that the several officers under this charter should "receive for their services out of the city treasury, a compensation to be fixed by ordinance, not to exceed four thousand dollars a year." The treasurer, however, might "receive in lieu of salary not to exceed one half of one per cent. on all moneys received, paid out, and accounted for by him, and the collector not to exceed one per cent. on all moneys collected and paid over." The mayor's and recorder's clerks should receive not over two thousand dollars a year, the clerk of the board of aldermen not over twelve hundred dollars, and the assessor not over fifteen hundred dollars. The members of the common council were prohibited from receiving any compensation for their services.

These provisions regarding the management of the municipal finances are here set forth prominently, because, as already suggested, they constitute the main points of difference between the two charters. The adoption of the second charter and the election of the officers provided for in it, were the last steps in the establishment, under the authority of the United States, of a legitimate municipal government in San Francisco. The election occurred on Monday, the 28th of April, 1851. On the evening of May 3, the two boards of the common council met in joint convention to examine the returns, and report to the mayor the result of the election. The examination having been made, the mayor was instructed by vote to notify the gentlemen named of their election, and they were requested to meet in the City Hall and take the oath of office. On the same evening the common council adjourned *sine die*, and thus ended its disgraceful career.

www.ingramcontent.com/pod-product-compliance
Lightning Source LLC
Chambersburg PA
CBHW031455270326
41930CB00007B/1011